Argumentation in Education: Putting Argument to Work in Your Classroom

Jeremy S. Edge, PhD.

Jade-Clairmont Publishers

2015

First Printing: 2015

ISBN: 978-0-9966234-0-7

Jade-Clairmont Publishers
PO Box 464425
Lawrenceville, Ga. 30042

www.argumentationeducation.com

Argumentation in Education: Putting Argument to Work in Your Classroom

TABLE OF CONTENTS

INTRODUCTION

IT IS TIME TO TEACH STUDENTS TO THINK ONCE AGAIN

Epistemology-the study or a theory of the nature and grounds of knowledge especially with reference to its limits and validity-
Merriam—Webster's Dictionary

At the heart of every teacher, every school, every system, and every movement regarding education should be an epistemological base. A basic premise and belief informing why things are done, how things are done, and from what understanding do these motivations stem seems as though it would be a good place to start, and a positive way to drive, a movement or process. Without a driving ideology, processes and ideals can get blurred and confused. A clear and concise force, which is sound at its base, can be the only way for something real and true to be accomplished.

As we approach ideas which are new to us, we approach them with our belief system. That system, for educated people and for teachers who find themselves situated firmly in their content area, involves some belief about what knowledge is and how it is created. Each of our individual content areas has some variance of belief as to the basis for knowledge and understandings. It is from that epistemic heart that we teach our content. We teach the basis for our understanding of what our subject area means and what it has to offer. Do we teach that belief, though? Do we impart into our students the meaning behind our understandings and where they come from? Are the young minds in our classroom privy to where the knowledge we are teaching comes from? Do they really understand what it is to be a professional in the field we teach? If we are not teaching our students where knowledge comes from, what counts as knowledge, and the basis for what we are teaching and believing, then we may be doing them a disservice.

There is one teaching methodology that allows for content knowledge, epistemic understanding, critical thinking, and logical reasoning patterns to enter the daily processes of our student. There is one methodology with an epistemic base of constructivism that also allows for each individual content area to add the nuances of their belief system. The concept of scientific argumentation presents a structure for students to create and mold their own knowledge and interpretations. Scientific argumentation shows students a way to make meaning out of things that they do not initially understand. Students build capacity for improvements in literacy skills, metacognitive awareness, critical thinking and assessment, and the reasoning that will allow them to make their way through new and difficult subject matter and an ever changing world. Through the theory and practice contained in the forthcoming chapters, I will explicate a way to help student learn (or remember) how to think...and think at a high level. Enjoy!

Chapter 1

A Short Modern Era Background of Scientific Argumentation

When reading through this section, it may help to organize the development of argumentation along the lines of the ideas and thought patterns which have contributed to the overall conceptual progress of scientific argumentation.

Work to determine your own conceptualization of what scientific argumentation is and what it means to you.

Read critically and question my assertions as to important developments and people

The aim of argument, or of discussion, should not be victory, but progress.

~Joseph Joubert

One of the first things you might ask when approaching this volume is, "What is Scientific Argumentation?" This is a pivotal question, as it is not something that is discussed often in mainstream education or even in science education. A thorough understanding of argumentation will be absolutely necessary in order to use this as a classroom practice in any kind of effective manner. Scientific argumentation itself has become a topic of intensified research interest in the past decade. This research becomes increasingly important in light of both Common Core Standards and Next Generation Science

Standards and their inclusion of argumentation as a conceptual and
practical part of understanding and learning. The argumentative
encounters which scientists go through in order to construct what
scientific "knowledge" is, has been going on ever since intelligent
beings first sought to explain the world around them. The concepts,
practices, and mental acuity required to successfully argue a point or
idea go as far back as written history…and likely before. Dialectic
contentions, logic and its ensuing disagreements, and the idea of
rhetoric and rhetorical analysis are popularly associated with great
societies leading them towards their modern practices and great
accomplishments. For the purposes here, I will focus on more modern
conceptual history.

Argumentation is commonly accepted as being a part of what
scientists do in order to create, detail, and defend what science
knowledge is. Thomas Kuhn expounded on the idea of knowledge
creation through experimentation, development of theory,
argumentation to determine the most agreed upon theory, and the
process therein, that scientists go through in order to develop the
knowledge base that is currently accepted in the science community.
Argumentation amongst competing theories generates better science
and more competent scientists. As Kuhn's book *The Nature of
Scientific Revolutions* details, the processes of developing scientific
theory come to light as a crossroads of ideas. Those who have ideas
as to why the natural world is the way it is or behaves the way that is
behaves compete with one another to convince the scientific
community, or better yet the world, that their idea is the one that
makes the most sense and explains the behavior with the most
accuracy. Competing scientists argue their theories to prove accuracy
and correctness along with the ability to predict outcomes while they

also attempt to explain away others. When there is a general consensus, which comes only with data, observation, explanation of natural phenomena, and the prediction of natural behavior, a theory or law is born and scientific understanding is constructed. When a theory no longer explains all of the data, it must be changed and argued again. The intersection of theory and debate coupled with a thorough understanding of the data and evidence involved on multiple sides of an argument is what fuels the construction and creation of scientific understandings and law.

Essentially, as far back as explanations of the world around us have been developed, they have needed to be argued against competing theories. The names and places associated with theories and knowledge are not often fully representative of those who had a hand in the development of the theory. The

> The practices which make scientific argumentation effective for critically assessing situations, thoughts, evidence, and essentially any information or observations are also applicable to most any situation in which we may find ourselves.

complicated task of developing consensus scientific understanding, or for that matter consensus understanding in any field, is long and uncommonly demanding Not only do ideas slowly develop over a period of time, but those ideas are in constant competition with other views of the world. The consistent need to fully explain and convince are driving forces in the development of understandings, yet it is also the necessity of defeating other theories and paradigms which lead to more concise and specific theory. The process of arguing for one's own theory and idea is not the sole purpose of argumentation. The arguing against another is also essential. The complete understanding of competing theories is pivotal to the work of distilling how a theory explains data and observation. The full critical view and assessment of the entire theoretical playground in which one works must accompany a winning argument. A historical view of scientific canonical Law and theory would reveal this to be true throughout history. The witchcraft and wizardry that consumed the natural world for many periods in history can be associated directly with the inability or unwillingness to go through the process of critical thinking and complete understanding of the actual evidence others provide in their theories.

Argumentation and the basic processes that define its workings are not relegated exclusively to the sciences. The practices which make scientific argumentation effective for critically assessing situations, thoughts, evidence, and essentially any information or observations are also applicable to most any situation in which we may find ourselves. Argumentation is present in the study of literature and the people that create it. In addition to just literature, the thinking skills involved in argumentation can examine the consequences of the literature in question as it sits within the situations and time periods of its authorship. As we interpret author's purpose, use of literary devices, the meanings hidden (and not so hidden) in figurative language, and what is meant by the words we read, the skills of argument are present. In every composition and rhetoric class I have been a part of, students have read and interpreted literature. With your opinion as to the meaning must also come specific textual evidence. With the evidence comes the explanation as to where the connections are and how it leads to your conclusion. This is the basics of argumentation in action.

Also, as historians examine multiple accounts of situations, letters, journals, diaries, governmental records, and other written or oral history, they must use these same skills and competition of ideas to create the understandings of the past that we take to be historical "fact." The entire process of determining the substance of historical understandings is argumentative by nature. Evidence and observation are interpreted and interconnected with prior knowledge and an opinion as to what has happened is born. Fortunately this newborn opinion remains as such until others are convinced. The act of argumentation works to convince others until there is a consensus of some kind. Like science and literature, these unions of thought are challenged with consistency and must continually be defended with the same kind of thinking and skills that went into the original development of the idea. Scientific argumentation as a skill set might as well be called social scientific argumentation, as it fits just about any situation or content area.

In mathematics the ideas of argument are present as well. In the creativity of geometric proofs, Newton's development of new math to solve his physics problems, and the decisions involved to determine a methodology needed to solve any equation one encounters, we see argumentative style critical thinking. As the previous generation confronts the "new math" the same argumentative thinking and assessment skills are there to help construct the understandings that are needed to progress. However, when students approach math word problems, the skills of argument can be their most valuable tools. Students must decide on method, determine how the information fits the method, and then also decide if their solution is correct in terms of what the problem is asking and how the answer fits the question. Quite simply put, the skills that we, as teachers, wish to

impart on our students are the skills that we find in the heart of
argumentation.

Moving forward, we can examine some of the instruction that
has been published in the area of argumentation. Even though many
processes are common to real world science and to the development of
scientific understandings, some have focused on getting the basics
down on paper, which is helpful in applying those techniques across
multiple content areas. Even though many of the processes have
multiple incarnations and alterations depending on their usage, as far
as scientific argumentation is concerned, the following relate what
many in the field see as important texts, ideas, and publication.

> *Quite simply put, the skills that we, as teachers, wish to
> impart on our students are the skills that we find in the
> heart of argumentation.*

Before continuing it may be prudent to distinguish specifically
between my conceptions of scientific argumentation as opposed to
debate. Essentially I consider scientific argumentation to be solely
based in data and evidence. Evidence can take on the form of theory,
scientific law, first person observed data, and previously or published
and peer reviewed observed data. I see debate as a more socio-
scientific argumentative device in which emotion, commonly accepted
ideas, feelings, and thoughts can be substituted for facts. Although
scientific argumentation and socio-scientific based argumentation both
have their place in classroom setting and within instruction regarding
argumentation as a skill, scientific argumentation is my main focus
and still applies to most educational settings.

Toulmin Argument Structure

Claim:

Thus gives your position and it is what you will be supporting or arguing.

Data/Evidence:

Facts, experimental results, confirmed observations, canonical information from content area, similar cases/examples, etc. which support the initial claim.

Warrants:

Specific reasoning to show how the data/evidence specifically lead to and support the claim.

Backing:

Information or support to show why the warrants are legitimate, why the sources are legitimate, and why they should be believed or trusted.

Qualifiers:

May be necessary to show what situations or cases the claim is relegated to, when/if the claim is situational. The qualifiers show the limitations of the claim.

The basic frameworks used to analyze the structure of arguments come from two fundamental sources. Toulmin made a case for the environment in which an argument is generated and the mental state of the arguer. He made reference to the power of words and the ways in which language is used in argumentation to allow for the structure and force of an argument. He was also clear that one must admit to the possibility of alternatives in order for it to be considered an argument. This is an important point for defining the argumentation process at its basis, as a person who does not truly consider the alternatives, or even the fact that there are alternatives, is not arguing a point, but is merely exposing an idea. The details of specific structural pieces that make up an argument are the most used portions of Toulmin's conceptual framework for argument. We will examine the language and usage portions of argumentative theory and research a little later. Toulmin's explanation of the structure and pieces of an argument are the starting point for many as they set out to teach students about argumentation.   Toulmin described the structure of an argument to include: an assertion that gives a position, a claim that supports that assertion, data to support the claim, warrants to show how the data can lead to the claim, backing to the warrants that show why they are legitimate, and qualifiers that may be necessary to express what situations and conclusions the argument is valid with. Qualifiers may contain rebuttals that would show cases and situations where the claim itself would not be warranted.   Later in this chapter, we will examine a specific example of each piece of the argument structure. When I teach argument, I do not incorporate the idea of qualifiers, as they represent specific cases. In general, I am teaching basic premises and practices of argumentation and thus qualifiers for specific situations are not necessary. In a more thorough and complex course on argumentation, I would include the fact that there are some arguments that are case specific and might vary situationally, such as in many astronomical physics intersections.

The framework as outlined by Toulmin is one that is good for looking at the structure of the argument. Arguments can be taught and evaluated with regard to the way they are put together and the inclusion of their necessary parts. The fundamental pieces of argument and the way that they are put together are necessary base structures for students to have in order to progress in their use of argument. Each piece is important in its own right and they each contribute to the whole that is the overall argument. The structure and the way in which arguments develop are somewhat like an art form and each individual part leads to the strength and perception of the overall resulting argument. The ability to create an argument and the presence of arguments in dialogical interaction can be measured within a framework drawing on Toulmin's conceptual basis. Thus once

Some Basic Reasoning Patterns as Detailed by Walton (1996)

Argument from Analogy

-Linking an argument to other situations where similar or the same reasoning can be applied

Argument from Precedent

- Arguing in regards to a specific case where an exception to a rule has been applied

Argument from Consequences

-Arguing causation based on your claim and the consequences either good or bad

Argument from Expert Opinion

-Showing experts or professionals in the filed agree with your premise and the application of your evidence

Argument from Popular Practice

-Arguing that a significant amount of people in the population are already doing what your claim supports

students have created arguments, we as teachers and the students as peers have a solid framework to evaluate those arguments. I have concerns with how to examine, teach, and evaluate counterclaims along with general lines of reasoning within an argumentation analysis based solely on Toulmin's structure. Toulmin's framework exhibits weaknesses in teaching and examining the reasoning and critical nature of the arguments formed. Thus the next major contributor to argumentative theory is important to relieve the shortcomings with reasoning patterns in Toulmin's argument scheme.

Walton asserted a framework that looked at the presumptive reasoning patterns that comprise arguments. He was concerned with the reasonable nature and effectiveness of arguments. Students and teachers must be able to assess the reasoning through which an argument accomplishes its goal of persuasion. Walton outlined twenty-five main argument schemes and provides critical questions in order to aid in deriving an argument's purpose, reasoning, and effective premises. A teacher using Walton's reasoning structures for arguments can elucidate lines of reasoning and justifications students may use in their arguments to help evaluate their appropriateness. In addition, students can use the reasoning patterns as a guide to help develop the reasoning skills and critical thinking necessary to attack reasoning in others' arguments. Walton's reasoning patterns will be outlined in detail later in this volume.

> *One must critically assess the many sides of any situation in order to create a thorough explanation, show causation, and defend their theory against attack from those alternates.*

Practitioners and researchers Kelly and Takao have developed a framework that deals with the epistemic levels of argument that rates the support an argument has and its factual and evidentiary basis as its justification for reasoning. Once students and teachers dive into the true meaning of what knowledge and understanding is within their content area, ideas as to the inclusion of content knowledge in arguments become more useful for teaching argument and evaluating student products. Epistemic levels begin with what are considered low quality arguments containing only data as support for claims, and continue to high epistemic level claims that use predominantly theory as their basis. Each successive level of inclusion of factual basis in the argument receives a higher ranking. These kinds of frameworks allow for more simplistic rating of arguments by teachers and student peers. Including these kinds of ratings in rubrics also details the expectations of high evidentiary and accurate evidence and reasoning in arguments. Such a framework might look like the following:

1.   ***Insufficient content knowledge***

2.   ***Incorrect content knowledge,***

3.   ***Non-specific content knowledge or general
     knowledge***

4.   ***Specific and correct content knowledge***

Deanna Kuhn, in her book *The Skills of Argument*, examined both the structure of argument and the reasoning involved together to help develop an understanding of what skills arguers need to possess. The actual thought processes and patterns of the individuals were dissected and appropriated to their respective connections to the argumentative process. Through this process of dissection and scrutiny, Kuhn could map the development of reasoning, causation, and the practicality of evidence within that the participants included in her study. I attempted to work in a similar way with students within my classroom with outstanding results. I will shed more light on that experience in a later section. The reasoning patterns and tendencies of people when confronted with situations that required participants to critically examine evidence, consider the input that led to their ultimate decisions or moral stances, support their final decision, and rebut opposition, led Kuhn to conclusions based on the average person's ability to argue effectively.

Kuhn was able to develop a baseline of abilities with which the general population tends to argue. She examined the tendencies of her participants to use certain kinds of evidence when seeking causation and noticed some alarming trends. First, most of the people in the study lacked the ability to actually assess the evidence that they used as far as the level to which it was believable and powerful. This shows their lack of ability to think critically about what they are examining and the causation of events and ideas. People were often confused about whether something was evidence or merely a restatement of their causal theory. One of the most important skills that a person needs in order to develop an effective argument is the ability to assess why they believe their evidence of causation to be true. This requires a person to think about what they believe and at the same time, why it is they believe in their evidence. The tendency to use emotional pleas and appeals to personal moral codes without regard to data or observational based evidence seems somewhat disturbing. In many cases Kuhn found causation was simply attributed to covariance or correlation of events and correlated change in the situations examined. Thorough evidence was not presented or there was little scientific or true researched factual evidence involved in creating their arguments.

Kuhn also illuminated an observation noted by many in the field of research regarding argumentation- the counterargument and rebuttal are the most significant difficulties that arguers encounter. It is the counterarguments and the rebuttals that require the most intense use of critical thinking skills, as the arguer must see the other side of the situation or examine other plausible theories while at the same time examining their own evidence in greater detail. In order to successfully create an argument, one must examine and break down alternative theories. Kuhn noticed

> *One of the most important skills that a person needs in order to develop an effective argument is the ability to assess why they believe their evidence of causation to be true.*

specifically that many arguers do not even contemplate the fact that there is an alternative choice or explanation to the events that they examined.   To develop an effective argument which can withstand epistemological, evidence driven, and reasoning attacks, one must metacognitively analyze their own ideas, epistemological beliefs, the source of their data, and the reasoning patterns used to connect their data to their claim. It is through this metacognitive awareness that alternate theories and connections can be seen and the counterarguments are illuminated for the arguer.

One must critically assess the many sides of any situation in order to create a thorough explanation, show causation, and defend their theory against attack from those alternates. Each theory or possibility must be critically examined in order to thoroughly counter and rebut. Overall, this is a skill not generally present in anyone without significant training or practice in the metacognitive and critical thinking processes within their own decision making, or problem solving, tendencies.   It is glaringly obvious that the main skills and abilities which are purported to be necessary for scholastic and worldly success are the very ones that seem to be missing from the general population. These are the skills that school systems want their teachers to develop in their students. These are also the most difficult to define and teach. Many have been told to teach critical thinking and metacognition, but few have been instructed as to how to do so.

To reiterate, Thomas Kuhn detailed the idea of a scientific concept as something that is proven through debate and the arguments created, supported by observations and experimentation. In many social science fields the knowledge that has been acquired or agreed upon is constantly examined and "proven" over and over again. Facts are derived from the discussion that surrounds observation and experimentation while there is also an attempt to disprove those facts or prove alternate theories. With time, theories can be altered through further experimentation and debate centered on observation until at some points the entire concept may be revamped.

For students the discourse surrounding thought and fact is pivotal. Consensus knowledge comes from the act of argumentation. It is not enough for students to merely memorize facts. Students should be involved in their curriculum and the content at the base level of knowledge and understanding. Students should experience how these facts were determined and thereby will have a deeper connection to their education.

Through most experience the parts of an argument are generic. A basic premise of an argument is presenting a claim and also supporting that claim with evidence and information. Knowledgeable thought and practice provides the means for a person to construct a claim and defend it with observation, previous facts, and justification from others' experiences and writings. The claim is supported specifically by data and evidence. This data and evidence must be supported by warrants and backing. Warrants are there to show how the evidence can lead to the claim and the backing is there to show that the data and evidence are legitimate. Currently, many in the field of scientific argumentation working with K-12 grade students have combined the warrants and backing into one category referred to simply as, "reasoning." This is often for ease of instruction and evaluation. The claim that has been created must be connected to the data and to the evidence through a logical line of reasoning and the data itself must be proven to be legitimate in nature.   I feel as though the warrants can be referred to as reasoning in order to help students refer to their knowledge of Walton's reasoning patterns. I feel that the idea of backing belongs with the critical assessment of the data and evidence with regards to validity and the source of that information. The structure of the argument rests on the basis of experience and knowledge. The claim is supported and detailed as well as defended. Within the practice of science, there is also the construction of the counterclaim by others in the stream of discourse surrounding the original presentation of a claim. The idea is to create knowledge based on experience, communication, and defense of claims. The counterclaim represents alternative ways of looking at the facts presented. The discussion and thought that comes from examining a counterclaim can be some of the most influential thinking a student will do. There is a specific cognitive challenge in the construction of the claim and the counterclaim that is based in the writing, construction, and organization of the discourse involved. Through the use of argumentation, a deeper understanding of the concept is attained through reading, writing, thinking, and examining experiences, all in a critical manner.

My Early Application

In the introductory lesson in my 8th grade classroom my students set right to work on proving an idea of their own through the argumentative process that I had listed on the whiteboard. I took very little time defining each piece of an argument, as the plan was for the students to hash this out in their own minds and with me as we actually created our argument. This is an oversimplified example to illustrate the pieces spoken about above, as I will examine my experience in this and other classrooms later in this volume. After some discussion as to what "controversial" topic could be both appropriate for school and for the demonstration, we decided on the assertion (claim) that cheerleading is a sport. As we examined this idea, there were students who fell on both sides of the claim. Some were emphatically in favor of the idea, while others were opposed. At the same time, there were some that were not sure if they had ever thought about the idea before, and thusly had almost no opinion either way.   It worked out perfectly. (Of course it did, I helped to choose the topic.)   After we decided on the claim, we were now looking for evidence. As students began to contribute it was obvious that it was much easier for them to develop the reasoning and the evidence together in their minds. Some of the data included the following:

Evidence

- *There are sports-style Injuries*
- *There are competitions in which cheerleading is judged*
- *It is performed as a team*
- *Requires athletic-style abilities*
- *Uses muscles, reflexes, and mental acuity together*
- *Requires training*

As the students were thinking of the data/evidence, they were developing the reasoning at the same time. They were automatically trying to assert how the data/evidence connected to the claim and at the same time looking at the legitimacy as well. Although some of their reasoning was opinion based and also examined popular opinions, the basic premises were present in their thinking. An argument based on a social idea is obviously far simpler to develop than a true scientific argument, but this was an introduction. The students also came up with the following as their reasoning:

Reasoning

- *Injuries – If Doctor's reports show cheerleaders are suffering the same kinds of injuries and in the proportion as other sports, then it is a sport.*

- *If there are Team competitions sponsored by major sports corporations, professional organizations, and schools which are judged, rankings are given, trophies are given, and there are winners and losers are similar to other sports, then cheerleading is a sport.*

- *Anyone who has witnessed cheerleading or tried it themselves sees the requirement of specific abilities related to the use of muscles in specific ways, the training that must take place in order to use the muscles in certain ways, and the specific mental focus and concentration match the requirements of other sports.*

- *Requires training*

With the understanding that counterarguments and rebuttals are the more difficult pieces of the process, I did not introduce them at this point. The obvious choice for a counterargument would be that cheerleading is not a sport. The process of examining the counterargument should lead the arguer to the evidence and reasoning in support of that idea. Some evidence in support of the counterargument that cheerleading is not a sport may include things such as:

Counterargument: Cheerleading is not a sport

Evidence and Reasoning in support of the counterargument:

- **Injuries in cheerleading can be caused by inexperience and carelessness**
- **Cheerleading is not a sport because there is no professional league**
- **Cheerleading is not a sport because it is not in the Olympics**
- **Cheerleading is not a sport because people cannot make a living performing it**
- **Cheerleading is not a sport because the NCAA does not see it as a sport**
- **Cheerleading is not a sport because most examples could fall under the idea of gymnastics.**

This is where we look at the critical thinking aspect of the process. As the arguer examines the other side of the argument, they then look at rebuttal evidence and ideas which would disprove that logic. It is most effective to rebut all points in the counterargument. Some rebuttal ideas for this counterargument would be:

Possible Rebuttals

- *Injuries in many sports are caused by negligence-i.e. not paying attention and receiving a blindside block, swinging a baseball bat with poor form and injuring the back or neck, etc.*
- *There are professional cheerleaders for most pro football and pro basketball teams.*
- *Football is not in the Olympics and it is one of America's most prized traditions.*
- *Many sports to tot allow their participants to make their living solely from that sport-i.e. minor league baseball, soccer, softball, etc.*
- *The NCAA cannot have all sports in college. If, however, you argue that cheerleading falls under gymnastics, then that is indeed an NCAA sanctioned sport.*
- *Gymnastics is very different from cheerleading. Cheerleaders combine some skills that gymnasts have and completely diverge from other skills. Cheerleaders are meant to develop*

emotional support and appeal for something and this is very different from gymnastics.

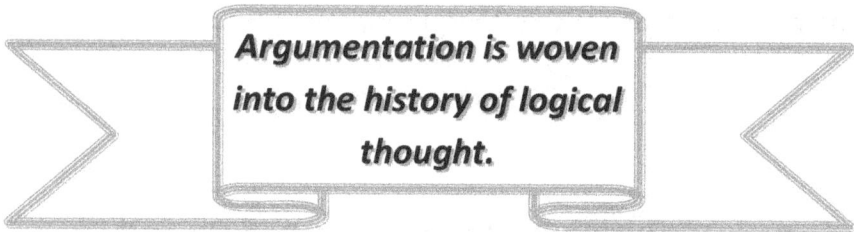

> ### *Argumentation is woven into the history of logical thought.*

With the full look at all sides of the proposal, the arguer would develop an argument that is stronger and less likely to be dismantled. Once again, this is a simplified example of scientific argumentation to allow for enough of a general understanding so that one may approach using argumentation as a classroom tool. Make no mistake, though; implementing scientific argumentation will be work. To get the true benefits, one should absolutely have the basic premises of argumentation interwoven in their general classroom practice. We will approach that throughout chapters 4, 5, and 6. The end of this short background of scientific argumentation, however, leads us to the theory that supports this process...and chapter 3.

In conclusion

Scientific argumentation is woven into the history of logical thought. It is the way that science is done by scientists as they determine what theory fits the data in the best way. Argumentation is how theory is created, accepted, and changed from time to time when necessary. The methodologies employed in decision making in government, in courts, and in our own personal lives are those of scientific argumentation. Good quality critical thinking is basically practicing argumentation. The basic scheme of argumentation has been examined, detailed, and laid out logically by Toulmin. Walton has examined the basic reasoning patterns that can be used to support and connect data and evidence to the ideas that are being argued, and Deanna Kuhn studied the ways in which everyday folks use these skills as they create and relate the opinions that they have on different kinds of topics. This is something that has been researched and developed to a level that now provides us as teachers with a fantastic opportunity to employ these methods in our classrooms with a sound basis and understanding of how these skills fit into the overall education of our students and the precise purpose for which we use these methods.

Chapter 2

The Ideologies Driving Argumentation

This is the section which provides the overall support for the ideology of scientific argumentation. Think about the following as your read:

1. What theories of learning are contributors to scientific argumentation?

2. Who are the driving forces in these theories?

3. Are these theories applicable to the modern era of education?

4. Do these theories fit with the epistemological beliefs that were ironed out in the Chapter one thinking exercises?

5. Do I support these ideas?

6. Does this fit my educational philosophy?

"Give the pupils something to do, not something to learn; and the doing is of such a nature as to demand thinking; learning naturally results."

— John Dewey

"A word devoid of thought is a dead thing, and a thought unembodied in words remains a shadow."

— Lev S. Vygotsky

In order to deepen the understanding an instructor needs to possess to appropriately teach not only the concept of scientific argumentation, but to also teach through the use of argumentation, we will now journey through the theoretical underpinnings of this approach to teaching epistemology. The frameworks that underlie the art of argumentation in education deal with how students learn and also how scientists, linguists, authors, mathematicians, historians, and many other professionals whose work involves cognitive thought, go about their work. These theoretical and conceptual frameworks span a range encapsulating such things as: the ideas of the cognitive development of children, the sociological dimensions of learning and knowledge, the epistemological concepts of knowledge, the philosophical ideologies surrounding scientific inquiry, learning, and discovery, the uses of language in learning and communication, socio-linguistic contributions to learning, and the structure and process of argumentation itself. When examining or venturing into the field of argumentation and how it is used to drive instruction, it helps to grasp these frameworks in order to understand how they inform the structure of this type of education as it has evolved through the recent decades. This research and these ideas are laid out to with the intent of showing support for my forthcoming methodologies regarding teaching argumentation.

What does Research Say About How Students Learn?

Students Learn Through Inquiry

The go-to researchers and authors at the base of many inquiry theories are John Dewey and Lev Vygotsky. They each have voluminous accounts of their research that are very interesting reading. Fortunately, multitudes of writers have spent significant time distilling their ideas making the base ideologies more accessible to the masses. Argument is clearly an extension of the inquiry based classroom experience and thus we can find some of the support for argumentation as a method of instruction in the support for inquiry.

In an inquiry-based classroom, students are afforded time and space to ask questions and derive answers through practices that involve acquisition of evidence that should help them in their development of understandings. This acquisition occurs in association with teacher facilitation that drives and encourages students to understand the concepts that will answer their questions about the world. Students are engaged in what is considered authentic learning because they direct learning through their own curiosity while developing skills necessary to quench their thirst for knowledge. Anyone who has had the experience of wanting to know or understand something has been curious. It is the learning that comes from the process of figuring the answers or the basis of a new concept that excites many people. A lesson learned from trial and error or a lesson learned "the hard way" as we make mistakes and struggle some is a lesson that often sticks with people for the longest time. Students in an inquiry activity often distill their ideas and the heart of a concept through the process and the social interaction that takes place with their peers and the facilitator. The experience of being immersed in an inquiry activity at the same time immerses the students in the world of whatever subject matter they are experiencing. This deepens both the experience and the effect of that experience. When we are looking for students to understand the nature of what they are learning, this manner of acculturation gives students the ability and the confidence to construct meaning in a subject area that they feel more comfortable in because it is a part of their personal world. Students internalize the concepts and ideologies central to the culture of the content that they are learning.

Inquiry presents students with a method of learning and knowing that is derived from experience and allows students to live their education. This form of learning prevents students from inheriting assumptions others have made about anything. As Dewey (1986) notes, "If we see that knowing is not the act of outside spectator but of participator inside the natural and social scene, then the true object of knowledge resides in the consequences of directed action," (p.157). Inquiry is at the heart of associating with the world around us, whether it is in the laboratory, where the direction of scientists that came before leads the way to new action, or in the classroom, where the teacher facilitates participation in inquiry activities in which scientific epistemologies are used to create knowledge. Each experience allows the learner to see the world in a new way and to build on what they have already known. Each individual act and activity changes the perception of the past activities and experience at the same time that it changes the way a students will approach future learning experiences.

> *Inquiry presents students with a method of learning and knowing that is derived from experience and allows students to live their education.*

Dewey and Vygotsky have also written extensively about the social nature of learning and the relationship to inquiry that can be found there. Along the same lines as learning lessons "the hard way," we tend to acquire information needed in social activities more efficiently because of the need and ability to contextualize these experience through the natural social nature of humans. As one member of the group begins an understanding, the rest can contribute and feel the need to keep up at the same time. Thereby the learning process is given a significant boost. Learning and knowledge are contextualized as a product of social and cultural environments in which education occurs. The values of society influence the terms of accepted knowledge. An argumentative approach to that knowledge allows the individual to develop their own ideas and values. With this, students find their own place in the world and from that place can critically assess what they believe to be knowledge and understanding. Through natural social experiences, such as discussion with their peers, students can develop their abilities. Cognitive abilities are practiced specifically during these kinds of interactions. Through argumentative inquiry, students become far more powerful.

More modern experience and research supports that idea that the most sincere way to approach learning something is to do that thing. How many times have you heard someone say that they learn best by doing something and not by listening to someone talk about it? The modern world is full of kinesthetic learners. This fits in well with the idea of inquiry education. The way to learn science is to do science; and the way that science is done is through argumentation. In science we seek empirical evidence through experimentation and observation, but the real work of building understanding and explanation of the physical world is done through argumentation. Argumentation forces an inquiring mind to question and prove ideas of any sort, even their own.

It is in physical and mental exploration through experience that mental acuity is attained in a way most similar to authentic practice in all content areas. Just as I have detailed specifically how argumentation fits into the world of science, each content area with their own epistemological beliefs approaches their subject knowledge with a need for proof and defense of their ideas. The modern student is not one to trust and believe simply because we say so. With the extensive access to information, and not all of it trustworthy, society has developed an approach that sees information readily available. If we as educators are to have students trust us and our teachings, the proof must be there because they can find an alternate idea or bit of data elsewhere. The experience of argumentation makes the learning and understandings real for the student and thus more solid in comparison.

Experiential education gives students some power over their own education. Power relationships are important in education. Classrooms in which the teacher has the power and children are agents to receive knowledge, lack authentic learning. When students develop power and interest while sharing in education, they are engaged and ready knowledge creators. Argumentation in education has the potential to give students

Through argumentative inquiry, students become far more powerful.

power while promoting the idea of experience in education. Student choice has been a driving force in my own classroom and argumentation gives more students multitudes of choice as to what ideas they support, how they choose to prove their ideas, their reasoning patterns, and what they believe.

Students Learn Through Social Interaction and Their Use of Language

During the development of my own theories and approaches regarding argumentation, Vygotsky's ideas regarding the Zone of Proximal Development (ZPD) have been pivotal. I see this idea as essentially reaching out to students where they are educationally and bringing them along to where we would like them to be. The idea of the ZPD is what I refer to as the struggle. You can hear my students and myself constantly refer to the fact that, "the struggle is real." Although this may also be a pop culture reference, in my classroom, the struggle is constant. The idea of the ZPD has students working at a level that is just out of their comfort zone. When students work with other students in pairs, small groups, and sometimes as a whole class, they are taking advantage of both the social nature of learning and helping to move others along in their own personal struggles. The concept of the social nature of learning supports the use of group discussion and dyadic conversation related to constructing argument and detailing ideas. As part of the ZPD, members of groups can help elevate each other to higher levels of learning, as some members will be at different levels of cognition concerning the material of study.

We use scaffolds to help students achieve things that they could not initially do on their own. They are struggling and sometimes suffering as they tussle with new information, ideas, and understandings. Through scaffolding, students are assisted using worksheets or guides, teacher assistance, peer assistance, or computer programs to complete tasks that they might not be cognitively ready to complete. Scaffolding gives students practical experience in completing tasks and is a commonly accepted way to assist the learner in: becoming independent, learning concepts that underlie tasks, and relating ideas cognitively to what they already know. Scaffolding, as a process, makes use of both background knowledge in an area and whatever schema learners have already developed to facilitate their understandings.

Piaget developed ideas regarding schema as a significant part of the way in which learners internalize new information and concepts. The schema that they build then allows them to make sense of other new ideas. Schema is a usable form of background knowledge or background conceptual understanding. Schema can be a method of approach or a similar understanding that learners already possess. As a student becomes more familiar with the terminology, approaches, and understandings of a field or content area, then they build more schema to understanding and learn both within that are and within other areas. The relationships between different semantic relationships can be highlighted more quickly as students understand the familial connections between concepts

> *The formation of a concept in the mind is a collective task of which language is pivotal.*

As students are struggling with information, many things are happening. Two of those things are likely that they are communicating with their facilitator and/or their peers and they are doing so while using language. In a socio-linguistic framework and view of learning, the communication and its predication on language are both key to the overall understandings that students develop. In many subject areas, vocabulary is a keystone to understanding the concepts of that content area. Many times, vocabulary words can represent entire concepts or large pieces of concepts. This symbolic nature of language puts pressure on both learners and teachers to quickly acquire those words. Students' active use of language and its symbolic nature allows them to create new schema and conceptual understanding. The discourse that takes place in the classroom during social activities like argumentation put students in a position to manipulate concepts with both internal and external dialogue. The thought processes within their minds and the verbal communication with other students who are grappling with the same concepts makes learning social and language based. The more students are interacting and struggling with the ideas and the vocabulary that is used to describe those ideas, the deeper their understandings will become.

Language, and its integral relation to learning, is fundamental to argumentation. The idea that argumentation is a process through which language is used to construct competing stances and their supportive evidence, sees language as a learning practice. The specific language of a content area is closely related to the meaning making that takes place in discussions about that subject matter. In order to understand an idea, one must speak the language of that idea. Argumentation requires a significant use of the language of content areas and to argue a topic or concept, one must use specific content language. As that language is used through the social interaction of argumentation, deeper meaning and understanding arises. Both the internalization and the semantics of the content progress as one argues a claim. The arguer is immersed in the attitude of whatever content area they are arguing in, the social interaction of that content, and the values that thinkers in that area hold. As a facilitator during the discussion in a classroom, the teacher must pay close attention to the language that students are using. Herein lies the opportunity to encourage the use of content area and augmentative vocabulary words to be sure students are working with correct and appropriate schema.

Students Learn Through the Work of Constructivism

Knowledge is constructed through the actions that take place in the real world fields that are represented within the walls of the classroom and the expanse of the learner's mind. It is fundamental in the field of argumentation that acts of critical discourse along with dialectic (argumentative logic) and dialogic (discourse or discussion) interactions are the ways in which we create knowledge. So it logically follows that in order for students to be acculturated into the fields which they are constructing knowledge, they should work in the same manner as those in these fields. Scientists create understandings through experimentation and the argumentative process in which

> *The socio-linguistic nature of learning and communication is the glue that holds the argumentation methodology together.*

they attempt to prove their theory is most accurate. Those in the social sciences work in similar fashion by examining evidence of behavior, both past and present, and then working to convince others of their theory or explanation. Mathematicians work to show that their approaches or applications of theory are most accurate. Social scientists work to prove the validity of their various ideologies. Each core content area constructs knowledge in way that can be shown to subscribe to a constructivist point of view.

The idea is for students to construct their understandings as they experience what they are learning. When students participate in argumentative sessions, they are deriving not only the targeted knowledge, skills, reasoning, and general understandings that the school has deemed important, but they take a step further into the base traditions and nature of each subject area in which they are working. Theoretically, the learner becomes a part of the real world of each content area. This kind of holistic learning allows for multiple intelligences, learning-styles, and ability levels to actively engage and build new knowledge that they can own integrate into an overall scholarly knowledge base.

To Summarize and Conclude

The theoretical basis for scientific argumentation is well researched and thoroughly entrenched in educational experience. Amidst Dewey's ideas and practical application regarding inquiry based learning we find that multiple modern day educational researchers and theorists have taken up the charge of learning through experience and working with real word issues. With each new experience, a broader base of tools and understandings to use and apply to every other experience is molded in the minds of our students. Epistemologically, the idea of constructed knowledge and the creation of our own truths based on these theories works to support what many might call an "old school "method of teaching. Let's talk about it some and let's get to doing it. Many call this kinesthetic learning and more and more we see that the modern day student learns through doing. I know I do.

Moving on to Vygotsky and the idea of the zone of proximal development, it is plain that scientific argumentation is perfect for bringing students to the edge of their comfort zones and taking them one step over so that they struggle. When students struggle with information and skills, they are learning. If they got everything right and did everything right, then what would we actually be teaching them? Group work, teacher modeling, and scaffolding are all important for learners as they struggle to build new understandings in various content areas. Vygotsky realized that students need to practice and work their way through to mastery levels. Careful design of scientific argumentation based thinking and learning will do just that for our students.

The socio-linguistic nature of learning and communication is the glue that holds the argumentation methodology together. Vygotsky understood the linguistic interactions that group discussions and social learning foster within students. Language is the way that we communicate and the method that our brain uses for thinking. As students communicate socially about the ideas they are struggling with, those ideas become more clear and a part of the students' schema for learning and interpreting the world. Jay Lemke also saw the literacy connection with learning. The words that we use represent the concepts that we are learning. For students, learning to speak in the language of learning and communicating in the language of the subject matter they are studying is at the heart of the thinking and communication involved in argumentation. Reading and interpreting new ideas and relating them to prior experience are necessary in order to create arguments. Critically assessing the sources of those ideas and the specific worlds in which those sources situate themselves in creates the necessity of critical thinking, metacognitive awareness, and more communication. The writing portion of argumentation solidifies, organizes, and distills the thinking that students must do at a high level in order to be successful. It is when writing is woven throughout the content areas that the greatest thinkers we can educate become influential to the next generations.

Chapter 3

Why it Works and What it Develops in the Learner

Hear one side and you will be in the dark. Hear both and all will be clear.

- Thomas C. Haliburton

As you read through this chapter, think about your teaching styles and practices.

Try and imagine if these benefits are something that you want to see in your classroom.

Ask yourself if these assertions are things you can or need to improve on in your teaching.

If you want to begin here, start imagining places in your lessons that literacy and critical thinking skills are already needed or used.

Think about where group work and class discussions are appropriate already in your classroom.

Examine your modeling, think-aloud, and scaffolding methodologies. Imagine how you will include these new ideas into your current methods.

Ask yourself what your idea of critical thinking is.

Determine what you think metacognitive awareness includes

For students and teachers alike, the processes of scientific argumentation in some ways force everyone involved to dig deeper into whatever is being taught. In order to create an effective argument, one must have a full understanding of the subject matter in question and at the same time must also understand what has gone into the theory or line of thought at hand. Whatever the topic, it has to be examined from multiple points of view in order to create the type of argument that will stand up to educated scrutiny. In short, the act of creating a sound argument involves copious amounts of skills based in literacy, writing, critical thinking, and metacognition. Success with argumentation also requires a certain amount of grit on the part of both students and teachers. The rigor of creating scientific arguments more often over a period of time will surely hone these skills to a level of proficiency that would make any school or teacher proud (and jump for joy). As we have seen the theory in support of argumentation, we can now take a look at the reasons how and why applying that collection of theory actually works.

Literacy

Literacy is an important part of all life in the modern world. There is a constant barrage of text to be discerned in the life of those in the 21st century and it does take some skill in order to understand and function in this world and within that text. Language itself brings each culture together and helps us relate to one another in a specific way. This allows us to create social connections that are specialized for our individual networks. The idea of literacy in school and society revolves around all of the way in which we communicate multiple kinds of information. Here, the idea of literacy will represent reading and writing in order to communicate, organize, and construct ideas and knowledge. Literacy as a concept can be represented by the cultural methodology surrounding these types of communication and thinking. With literacy, the world can be understood, navigated, and enjoyed; understood through communication and interaction, navigated through instruction and direction, and enjoyed through countless forms of entertainment and pastimes. Literacy is not only important, but it is necessary for a comfortable and informed life. With this in mind, the development of these skills is a necessary part of the educational system. In learning literacy skills, there are those that are broad and encompassing, while there are also many that are specific to certain areas of life and education. Language itself is ever evolving and thus is constantly being created as the demand arises. As such, language allows us to use and manipulate it for the purposes of creating and understanding knowledge.

When approaching the topic of literacy across the curriculum in discussion involving schools, there seems to be a major push to explain why it should be done and how it is beneficial. The realm of literacy, reading, and writing across the curriculum seems to be split into several main ideas. The first of these focuses primarily on the improvement of reading and writing skills. For those who wish to include literacy skills in a classroom in any subject, copious resources exist to explain how to aid a student in learning to read, improving reading, improving writing skills, and overall writing activities. There are multiple studies that show how practicing literacy skills while you teach other subjects, increases a student's mastery level in those literacy skills. One of the major improvements shown has been with the acquisition of various reading and comprehension strategies as these strategies are taught and applied to multiple subject areas. Studies have shown that teaching multiple strategies and using these strategies in multiple content areas improves literacy skills and the ability to read and comprehend multiple kinds of text with varying topics and subject matters. The ability to use different strategies in order to comprehend different texts is a benefit of teaching and using these techniques across multiple curriculum areas. As a teacher who has taught most core areas and sometimes worked in a class teaching language arts and social studies simultaneously, I can attest to the fact that using strategies in multiple environments allows students to not only learn them more effectively, but also to see that strategies can be used in more than one area of both school an life.

In addition to reading and comprehending well within multiple areas, students who are inundated with literacy skills and strategies across content areas tend to develop skills that can be used in those content areas in order to develop understanding, locate and comprehend information, and understand increasingly complex vocabulary within a specific content area. The concentration on techniques specific to reading and comprehension allow for students to do more independent work and at the same time improve their overall reading and writing test scores. Through both professional development and experience, I have seen benefits when students are taught specific strategies to use before, during, and after a reading activity. In addition, the use of writing is important within these literacy skills, as there is minimal time within the walls of the classroom and the writing that students do can be reviewed with greater frequency than discussion within the class. Overall, with the push for teaching literacy skills within multiple content areas and a design that implements mainly comprehension, vocabulary, and more writing, the benefits have been clear as reading and writing scores have improved where this has taken place.

Students who participate in argumentation make good use of literacy skills in context. Almost all students at one point or another will find it necessary to use specific reading and comprehension strategies to work with difficult or high level informational writing. As learners use these strategies more often they not only become more comfortable with them, but they become better readers and writes overall. As they continue to add skills and information to their repertoire, their level of background knowledge and their available schema increase exponentially.

The prior knowledge and schema that students develop and bring with them is the foundation for understanding and constructing new. Everything that a student has read or experienced in school and beyond becomes important for the understanding of what others are doing and for the comprehension of a task. Creating models in the student's terms is pivotal in order to realize what is being learned. These models also depend on prior knowledge and experience. Through both what they read to understand and the models that they construct, students develop an understanding of how they go about their own work of constructing understanding, but also how their work is conditional to the work that others have done before them. Much of the learning that takes place in a school building is derived from the work of others, but through argumentation, students also get the opportunity to do some of that work themselves.

The languages of fields of study are developed through discussion and use within the field, and with that development of the language, such as vocabulary and conventions, is the development of the concepts that these vocabulary words are used to express.

Almost all discussion or discourse is effective in some way. With that development of language, such as vocabulary and conventions, is the development of the concepts that these vocabulary words are used to express. When the dialogue is on topic and facilitated well, I have always seen discussion as a pivotal way to develop content area understanding. Small and large group discussion allows a forum for learning and the manipulation of concepts. Discussion leads to concrete understanding of ideas, the transfer of knowledge, and the creation of knowledge through socio-cultural interaction.

In addition to discussion and argumentation, writing is a key part of literacy. Writing is the way in which field professionals communicate with each other and document their observations. Knowledge is written down in order to be collected and to be tested by others. Scientific knowledge specifically, is created through the development of theory and the testing of that theory by other scientists. Writing is the key method of recordkeeping for scientists. However, writing serves more than just the recordkeeping purpose. As I noticed quickly in my classroom, writing is a tool for constructing meaning and understanding. Through writing, one can develop a deeper connection to their work and organize their ideas in order to understand what is developing from them. Through various kinds of writing, such as reflective writing and journaling, questions can be worked out and answered through writing in order for the organization and derision of concepts from experience and ideas. Any English teacher can attest that there must be a mix of reading and writing in order to aid the thought process and to construct complex ideas. Writing is an integral part of the learning process and thus overall literacy.

Residing within the concept of argumentation, the actions of reading and writing, and the art of discussion in fields of content, a basic premise remains regarding language and its use. To build on the theoretical views about the socio-linguistic nature of learning and the benefits of dialogical interactions in the classroom, it should be clear that venturing into argumentation places language and discourse at the center of classroom activities. The consistent use of the words and concepts associated with any new idea will certainly allow for students to become more familiar, and more importantly,

> *Whether the amount of choice is large or small, many students perceive greater intrinsic motivation when there are options for them to make for their own learning path.*

more comfortable using the words and the concepts that they represent. As students become more comfortable with the words and concepts associated with argumentative thinking, then they think critically with more ease and frequency. Just like any other skill, the practice of using language in a certain way to develop and convey thoughts gets better with repetition.

Choice

A great many studies as well as personal experiences identify "choice" as a key factor in students' motivations within the classroom. In developing arguments, students have more access to choices as to their claim and the way in which they will support or refute claims and counterclaims. The choices students must make in order to develop their path are up to them and they can work with ideas or experiences that they are comfortable with. The argument, the evidence, and the specific connections are like a puzzle that students put together in their own way. Multiple possibilities always exist and students choose their path multiple times during each argumentative session. Whether the amount of choice is large or small, many students perceive greater intrinsic motivation when there are options for them to make for their own learning path. Overall, the fact that argumentation is a skill and not specific content to be learned lends itself to teachers and students having a greater amount of choice as to when to use argument and what the subject matter that they use it with.

Critical Thinking and Supporting Ideas

The idea of critical thinking centers on the way in which ideas are processed and organized. Critical thinking is not just an approach but a methodology. There are many differing definitions and approaches to critical thinking, but they generally have multiple processes and concepts in common. Much of what is detailed when discussing critical thinking is the process and the approach to thinking and discerning new information and ideas. I researched thoroughly as I tried to clearly focus and identify my own definition of critical thinking. In order to try and teach such a daunting yet increasingly important skill, I thought it was prudent to gauge the opinions of experts. Those expert opinions are detailed below and, as it was specific research, I have cited their work accordingly.

> **The critical thinker has an aspect of deduction that takes place as they process knowledge.**

Ruminskio and Hanks (1997) describe critical thinking as the approach of the thinker that leads to the development of new information, insight, experimentation, thought, and skeptical research. They describe the critical thinker as one who is curious, skeptical, relational, logical, persistent, open-minded, fair, and intellectually flexible.   Thus the skills developed by the critical mind look at information and determine if it is important and if it is reasonable. One who thinks critically manipulates information and compares it with what is already known. They are skeptical and yet open-minded at the same time. Information is not merely accepted, it is processed. Hinchney (2004) goes on to make the assertion that a critical thinker places the new knowledge in contest with their previously developed cultural knowledge, experiences, and assumptions. This consciousness of cultural expression in the formulation and contextualization of new information also leads to an understanding that those from other cultures may have different assumptions, thus leading to different socio-cultural contextualization.

Petress (2004) looks at critical thinking as an ability to explore a problem while integrating the experiences, information, and assumptions the thinker has into the process while still being able to justify one's outcome. In this design, the critical thinker consciously approaches new ideas and information in a well thought out way and with curiosity. According to Petress, the critical thinker determines relationships, categorizes concepts, draws conclusions, and must be able to recognize their own limitations, including any lack of knowledge, in the process. This leads to properly conceptualized new ideas.

Rudd (2007) speaks of critical thinkers as using specific processes as they think and having standards to determine what is and is not acceptable information. The process that they follow is reasoned and has a specific purpose in mind. The critical thinker has an aspect of deduction that takes place as they process knowledge. The reasoning affects how the information is categorized and whether it is seen as important or not important. Critical thinkers compare new information to what is already known and understood in order to categorize, accept, or negate it. The process is somewhat systematic as the critical thinker embraces the new and compares it with the old. Rudd described the critical thinker as understanding their own previously held assumptions and purposefully reflecting on them while developing new understandings. This reflection is an important part of metacognitive awareness and thinking.   Heath (2012) describes a similar process as new ideas are looked on with skepticism as to where they come from and who benefits from their acceptance. The critical thinker here is looking at power; who has it and who wants it. There is an examination of what perspectives are represented and which are left out. New ideas and information are closely examined in order to determine if a source can be trusted.

As can be seen above, all manner of critical thinking follows procedure and has a purpose. The development of new knowledge does not come without comparing it to old understandings and determining if it is quality fact or of it is opinion and conjecture. As described, critical thinking is systematic and involves reasoning, classification, and organization. In both the concepts of using literacy in content areas and being content literate, critical thinking is fundamental. In using literacy within learning, there is a constant use of background knowledge and understanding engaging the reader as they attempt to understand text and especially new vocabulary. In the writing process, ideas are classified and organized. In both reading and writing, the importance of reasoning patterns along with the sequencing of ideas and events must be precise in order to develop and communicate meaning. The processes of critical reasoning and creating a critical summary of text necessitate this systematic approach. In using literacy techniques to teach content, a critical thinking approach promotes and improves the connection students make with what they read and what they write.

Through the use of writing, (expository, persuasive, and narrative), information processing and organization takes place within the author. In my own life and in the experience of my colleagues, writing is a way of seeing problems and issues laid out on the page, which makes them far easier to solve. Information must be classified as to where is goes in the structure of text and the importance level of that information must be examined as to determine its value for the solving of problems. Writing itself is a synthesis of ideas and can lead to better understanding through critical thinking. Writing also leads the student to understand and scrutinize their current level of knowledge and understanding. Through this process, previously held knowledge is connected with newer knowledge to determine if there is a thorough understanding. If not, the critical and metacognitive thinker must find more information in order to develop a complete grasp of the new concept. This reflection is a pivotal part of critical thinking.

Learning is a process and a way of reasoning and this way of thinking should be critical in nature.

Content area literacy itself demands critical thinking skills and processes in order to develop meaning. It is unlikely that a student would be able to develop the kinds of arguments and apply previously held understandings to the contextualization of new knowledge without using the aforementioned critical thinking skills. This literacy requires the development of arguments in order to relay the thinking and understanding of the experiences, ideas, and theories of the field of study for the student. This complex task calls for examining evidence and for classifying that evidence within the argument according to its importance as well as influence. The thinker must examine this evidence systematically in order to create the argument. Information must be scrutinized as to its validity and credibility with regards to current observation and past information. The student has to comprehend what level of knowledge they have and what level they need in order to construct the argument and the quality of that information should dutifully be determined.   The construction of claims and counterclaims is based on these processes and is critical in nature. Argumentation is a way to use and develop critical thinking skills.

The discourse of any content area as illustrated previously in examining scientific literacy is a constantly evolving process that itself also demands critical thinking. The speech of content areas, and school in general, becomes the creation of new knowledge. The thinker is obligated to examine the

The metacognitive thinker understands what a learning situation calls for in terms of strategy for understanding and approaches the experience with a useful strategy.

observations, explanations, and conclusions that they draw in order to be able to refine their ideas in discourse. The idea of discourse itself seeks to examine and dissect one's own ideas along with the ideas of others. As professionals communicate, their thought and ideas are at all times available for scrutiny and critical examination. Writing in all content areas is also a cumulative affair. Content area canon and text is an accumulation of facts and discoveries which those in the field are constantly adding to and scrutinizing. Learning is a process and a way of reasoning and this way of thinking should be critical in nature.

Metacognitive Thinking

The idea of metacognitive thinking revolves around the thinker themselves and knowledge of their personal thinking processes. Metacognitive thinking is essentially a way to self-monitor learning. The learner must be aware of what processes they are using, perhaps being aware of their critical thinking systems, and be able to regulate which processes they are using for what purpose. This involves knowing multiple strategies and understanding their use situationally. The metacognitive thinker understands what a learning situation calls for in terms of strategy for understanding and approaches the experience with a useful strategy. These thinkers understand that they are a part of the thinking process and as such must be actively engaged in their learning in order to be successful.

Metacognitive thinkers also understand that learning itself is a mental process that must be thought about and focused on. I consistently work with my students incorporating metacognitive self-awareness as they complete assignments. I assure them I have planned my lessons with purpose which ultimately may be missed by a "sleep-learner." One who thinks and works metacognitively focuses and concentrates on the task at hand while they are determining the strategies needed to complete that task. Thus, like critical thinking, metacognitive learning and thinking takes more effort and focus than merely copying definitions or answering basic recall questions. The skills required for critical and metacognitive thinking can be taught, but at the same time the learner must remain focused on the task and put forth more effort. As the metacognitive thinker approaches learning, the tasks that they undertake and the thinking which they employ lead to better learning outcomes because in order to work metacognitively, the learner must monitor what they are learning and, more importantly, if they are learning.

In teaching literacy practices, metacognitive strategies are important for comprehension. A good reader who comprehends what they are reading and can internalize the knowledge contained in text must constantly monitor their understanding. They do this through understanding what strategy is needed for each scenario they find themselves in. Consequently, a significant part of literacy training is teaching these strategies and the situations in which they are effective.

> **Metacognitive thought plays an important role in their internalization of the learning process**

Also, as literacy is used in the content areas, journaling as a learning and reflective technique can be of utmost importance. The art of journaling encourages students to think about what they are learning and a proper prompt will have the student considering how and why they are learning it. This is at the heart of metacognitive thinking. Incorporating journaling is, of course, another strategy that can be used as a metacognitive tool. Students can journal to maintain direction through their process of creating knowledge as well as track their progress.

As a learner is immersed in content area literacy, the process of metacognitive thought plays an important role in their internalization of the learning process and its goal. Perhaps the most cognitively challenging part of a literacy-based style of teaching is the concept of argumentation. Creating claims and counterclaims as well as locating and expressing the evidence needed for these is a strenuous mental process. The selection of strategies needed to do this well is metacognitive in nature. Students involved in creating arguments must know what strategies to use in each situation and must monitor their own progress as the argument is created. The idea and processes of challenging and questioning the ideas of others is at the heart of argumentation. Approaching and organizing multiple tactics and sets of data, including a wide range of texts, in order to be able to critically examine ideas requires multiple approaches that are managed through metacognitive thought. Processing new understandings through the deduction of facts from a set of multiple sources and claims requires differing approaches. Distilling ideas from sources that must be sifted through in order to determine a stance with the most support is a substantial task. Focus and self-reflection are pivotal in argumentative sessions that ask students for this kind of thinking. Once again, these multiple processes are managed through metacognitive reasoning and management of strategies, processes, and information.

Within both the use of literacy in education and content area literacy, there are specific approaches and strategies which are taught to students in order to be used. With this instruction should come the metacognitive teaching as to when to use the strategies and techniques taught. Whether it be reading or writing, the student must be able to approach the activity with their intrinsic motivation and understanding of the processes in order for learning to take place. The teacher cannot constantly lead the learning; the student must direct their path. This is what metacognition entails. A best practice in aiding students with their critical thinking and metacognitive development is the art of scaffolding.   Scaffolding is a part of metacognitive instruction and teaching in both literacy techniques and scientific literacy. It is important for teachers to model he kinds of thinking and approaches necessary for success so that students can see this thinking in action. It is crucial for teachers to allow students into their minds to see how a critical and metacognitive thinker approaches new information and tough problems. Within the development of the previously mentioned reading and writing skills that are used in literacy strategies as well as scientific learning, scaffolding as modeling and thinking out loud is a part of the teaching strategy in order to develop the skills desired in students.

Social Aspects

As students work individually and in groups of varying sizes, my experience and research shows that the social aspects of the argumentative process lead to better outcomes. I previously detailed the theory behind the social nature of learning and knowledge acquisition. Essentially, as students actually

> *Groups work together toward a single goal, and at the same time bring varying amounts of experience and background knowledge to a situation.*

talk about what they are trying to learn and make the experience a social one where the good of the group depends on actually fully understanding the concepts, then the students attain, and retain, concepts better. When a student has to talk about something and possibly teach someone else or help them to fully understand, then learning becomes more meaningful to each individual as well as the group.

Also, one of the key parts of argumentative instruction and practice is the social aspect of argument and learning to argue. Building on previously stated ideas, the social aspect of language and learning has been researched thoroughly. When students are talking about the information they are attempting to master, they are thinking about it more. If students are engaged in meaningful discussions with a purpose, then they generally increase the likelihood of successful assimilation of information into long term understandings. Argumentation allows for those meaningful discussions. Students can work in small groups of two, three, and four to develop their arguments. With multiple viewpoints represented in the group, the likelihood of examining a claim from many angles is greater. One of the main goals of using argumentation as a teaching tool is this kind of varied viewpoint attack that leads to a more critical assessment of the topic at hand. Groups work together toward a single goal, and at the same time bring varying amounts of experience and background knowledge to a situation. The social aspects of argumentation truly bring the pieces of language and social learning together for the best results.

Winning!

In my experience, one of the most prominent motivators I heard from students as they developed their skills at argument was the fact that they loved to be right and to win. In many cases, the sole motivation was to win the argumentative session and have their ideas heard. In the age group inclusive of middle and high school students, they are often going through stages in their lives when they feel muted or unimportant. The act of argument gives a voice to these students and allows them to be successful and prove that they have what it takes to be something special.

In Summary and Conclusion

Literacy in education is a common theme with many educational movements. The ability to read and write is possibly the single greatest set of skills a person can have in this world. I have always held the belief that if a person can read for comprehension well, then they can teach themselves anything. If you add in the skills of critical assessment of what you read, then you are not easily fooled because you are truly an individual thinker. Teachers would love to have well-read students who can pinpoint their ideas and deliver them in multiple well organized paragraphs. In the task of reading, prior understandings are always brought to each individual experience with text. Through the argumentative process, students are almost constantly reading and writing in order to develop their own ideas, present those ideas, analyze the ideas of others, and distill everything that they have been through. Practicing literacy skills with consistency in everything students do will absolutely develop the critical reading skills that they need. If these literacy techniques are used everywhere in the building through something that is not necessarily called literacy or reading, but instead is woven into the entire scholastic process, then that is how it will be perceived. School will equal literacy and thus so will life. During the argumentative sessions students develop schema, summarize their learning for themselves and their group-mates, see multiple points of view, and associate new knowledge with everything that they already know.

Argumentation brings with it two things that research shows students work for: discussions and choice. The literacy piece of argument flows into the social communication aspects. Students tend to learn and retain more when they discuss it. In small groups, pairs, and whole class group discussions students spend a significant amount of time communicating and they spend nearly all of their time engulfed in literacy practices. At the same time, students have differing amounts of choice as they work their way through arguments. Even though they may not have control of the topics of their arguments (though I believe there are controversial issues to be attacked in all subjects which can incorporate the necessary content knowledge) they may have control of their stance within the topics. Students are constantly making choices that determine the outcome of their sessions. As they realize, possibly with our help, how much control they have and that with every experience and each new word they read and learn that they have increasing control over school and their lives, their engagement increases.

Where we get the most "bang for our buck" in argumentation is in the critical thinking and assessment of what students are reading. During the research process and the expanded argument development process, students must see everything from multiple angles while and the same time questioning the motivations and validity of where they are getting their information. Critical thinking is a major piece in decision making and developing opinions. There is no way to create a successful and complete argument without critically assessing multiple facets of what students are doing. As they practice and we model and scaffold for them, we can pull them through the ZPD and have them independently thinking within the time we have them. If students are critically literate when they leave our classrooms and schools then we have succeeded at the highest level.

The questions that student must ask themselves as they read critically and develop their argument are training for thinking about how they are approaching subject matter and really just thinking about their own thinking. Students can develop their own process for approaching their thinking and learning. As they understand what it takes to be successful in their own progression, they can develop, once again with our help, the questions that they must ask themselves and the guideposts that keep them on track with their learning. Their literacy approaches and cognitive awareness for what is necessary contribute to their metacognitive practices and their overall learning. Students can self-diagnose, self-motivate, and self-correct their own processes by seeing what works and what does not. Learning is a focused mental practice that requires distinct thinking about how they are thinking. If we can give them the trifecta of literacy, critical thinking, and metacognitive awareness, then they will be successful in whatever they attempt in the classroom.

Chapter 4

My Wonderful Experience in the Science Classroom

As you read though my experience with scientific argumentation and my students, try to think of your successes in the classroom and how they make you feel.

As you get a little more of an in-depth snapshot of what scientific argumentation looks like in a classroom, begin to think more cognitively about applying these practices in your classroom.

Ask yourself if you can see yourself venturing into my practices.

Develop some mental images of yourself involved with students in similar ways.

The difficult part in an argument is not to defend one's opinion, but rather to know it.

~Andre Maurois

Throughout my search for better ways to reach and teach my students I powered through multiple research proven strategies and ideologies. As I taught math, science, social studies, and language arts to middle and high school students, I found that the literacy aspect of thinking and learning always gave me the best results. This coupled with as much practice for any concept that we could possibly approach together allowed my students a level of success that always made us all very proud. Perhaps the greatest triumph, though, was finding topics that were interesting enough to make the most defiant, lazy, or struggling students work hard... and...learn.

The adventure that led me to scientific argumentation began quite naturally. With my degree in history and political science, I taught social studies for some time in a middle school. I loved teaching social studies and all that it involved. There were struggles along the path, as there always seem to be, and many of those struggles revolved around my students' issues with reading and writing properly. With the invitation to try new things in the classroom that was an obligatory part of NCLB, I soon found myself in an interesting situation. I would have the distinct pleasure of teaching in an ESOL inclusion class. With the incoming accountability for all students, it would be necessary to forget the idea of sheltered classrooms where ESOL students could take their time with the acculturation process and focus on language, both the social and academic varieties, rather than solely content. So there I was with multiple students who did not speak much English, some students who spoke almost no English, students who seemed proficient in English, and some students who seemed as though ESOL was a misnomer for them. It did not take me long to learn what the "experts" meant by the difference between academic and social English. It seemed many of my students would converse easily and thoughtfully in English that they mastered through everyday interactions, however, the language of science and social studies seemed far out of their reach in the classroom. I looked any and everywhere for those "experts" to help my students find success.

It was during this year that I worked with an amazing young teacher fresh out of college. She was a language arts teacher but had done her student teaching working in a social studies class at the level that I was teaching. The more we interacted and talked about our work in the classroom, the more we noticed the crossover between our issues with the same student population. Also, we saw the connections with our strategies and methodologies. Finally, we decided to combine our efforts into one class. We taught social studies using language arts methods and we taught language arts through reading and writing about social studies topics. Students exceeded everyone's expectations (including their own) as they grasped the concepts and ran with them. Literacy practices and expertise on the part of the students seemed to lead to success in every class in which we implemented this concept. I decided that if students could read and write well, then they could accomplish anything they wanted and learn anything that they needed. Of course this only lasted for a short time. As the sands shifted so did the hearts of the powers that be. The great minds in the crystal towers decided the language arts department needed more men so why not move the man with the history degree over to teach writing? Suddenly there I was, teaching language arts to ESOL students.

No problemo.

Fate is not always a cruel taskmaster. At the same time that I was being converted to a language arts teacher, there was a leadership change and my social studies mentor from my first foray into teaching was coming back to social studies. Our rooms were connected by a collapsible wall. It only took little convincing for us to begin teaching in essentially the same way as I had before, but with me now in the role of the language arts teacher. I did not know how much I would love teaching literature and social studies at the same time. It was far more involved from the stance of the language arts teacher than my previous experience, but I was up to it. Overall the experience was just as wonderful as it had been the first time.

Success was a word that we used quite often in descriptions of our students' work. Fortunately for my future, I learned more than ever the importance of literacy skills and the acts of building those skills. Finding and using new practices for developing reading, writing, and speaking prowess became a part of my life that many came to refer to as an obsession. I couldn't help it, I have an addictive personality. Overall, though, I loved it so much that I did not have to think twice about continuing my graduate studies after I completed my master's degree. I jumped right into a Ph.D. program focused on literacy.

Now, I told you that story to tell you this one.

At the outset, my foray into scientific argumentation derived from my graduate work. I was focused intently on literacy across the curriculum as I tried to convince others in my school that it was a good idea. I was being somewhat successful with the principal when again I experienced the pangs of disappointment. My principal was relieved of his leadership duties. As I am sure you have predicted (as you have your conversation with the text), his replacement was far less interested in my desire for cross-curricular same classroom teaching methodologies. So with one swipe across my world, the progress I had made on selecting and researching a likely doctoral project disappeared. It was then with some candor that I approached my advisor with the need to spend some time collecting my thoughts on literacy and its application to my teaching, since my graduate work had always been with the desire to be a better teacher. So I took a semester and completed an independent study examining literacy practices in the middle school classroom.

As more chance events would have it, the attrition rate of my school was high and I soon began a path into science education that has led me to where I am today. During this time, I felt lost. My academic life and my work life had been all turned on end in a short time period. Through the guidance of my advisor and the in-depth research I conducted independently of a structured course, I wrote and wrote and wrote until I thought I had ironed out multiple ideas as to why what I had done in the past had been successful and how I could build upon that success to drive new research and methods for the betterment of educating students. My advisor suggested a book about literacy in science education which would change my life. The book itself helped to solidify my attachment to literacy practices and lead me in a direction in which I could transfer my old practices into my new subject area. At the same time, I found new and wonderful things to do in my classroom, too. Looking for more things that the authors of my favorite books had written

> *My academic life and my work life had been all turned on end at the same time.*

or contributed to, I came across a collection of knowledgeable authors: Jonathan Osborne, Sibel Erduran, Jay Lemke, Donna Alvermann, Deanna Kuhn, Shirley Simon, Rosalind Driver, Paul Newton, Bruno Latour and many, many more, through whom I came to know the idea of scientific argumentation. Here I really figured out how language and real scientific style activity should revolutionize not only science education, but education in general. BOOM! Life Changed.

As I reflect today, I am somewhat saddened that throughout my entire educational career as both a student from K-12 and then throughout decades in college (I went part time for much of my collegiate career) as well as a burgeoning career as a teacher, I had never heard of scientific argumentation until I was nearing the end of my education and was completely lost. Through essentially chasing any and everything down multiple rabbit holes, I found myself firmly planted in something I could believe in. I would rather it come later than never, though, so I dove in head and feet first (picture that if you dare).

After copious amounts of reading, theoretical soul searching, an epistemological epiphany, and everything else I could possibly do to prepare myself, I ventured into scientific argumentation in my classroom. The very first thing that I noticed was that I needed a very thorough understanding of scientific argument from top to bottom with regard to procedures, terminology, and the actual application of the methodologies. Actually creating lessons that would allow for the time constraints of my curriculum while at the same time teaching a concept that is at its heart a complete mash up of science, social sciences, and good old composition and rhetoric, turned out to be very labor intensive, especially if I had any expectation of successfully implementing them. My first foray ended with students and myself being frustrated and neither of us truly understanding what had happened. Each time we approached argument after that session, we were all exponentially more prepared. It was through the abject failure of early attempts at implementation that a few truths were highlighted.

1) Scientific Argumentation is RIGOROUS!

Students need to be truly prepared for the amount of rigor that is involved here. If you are of the opinion that students do not truly master concepts and content unless they struggle with them some, then you will love scientific argumentation. Students will likely start out below the level of thinking, reading, and writing that argument requires.

2) Scientific Argumentation requires CRITICAL THINKING!

It seemed almost impossible for students to be in any way successful without truly critically examining and assessing what they were reading and the sources from which they were reading it. Students had to develop an understanding of what made good information, good data/evidence, and most importantly what good scientific thinking was.

3) Scientific Argumentation leads to METACOGNITIVE EXPLORATION

Increasingly with every experience I witnessed, both visually and through eavesdropping, my students comprehending more and more that there were mental exercises that they had to follow in order to get where they needed to be. On many occasions it seemed as though they were developing the ability to coach themselves along the path to success (this of course took some amounts of time and tears)

4) We CAN do this!

It became readily apparent that I not only needed a full understanding of argumentation, basic reasoning patterns, and logic, but that I also had to really understand what I was teaching because we were going deep into whatever we studied.

So after the initial speed bumps of implementing something that I had not only never done in my own classroom, but at the same time had never seen anyone else do in their classroom, I approached the subject matter in a more scientific manner. I developed a plan and a fully functional way to implement that plan. I went back to the drawing board and examined what exactly my students needed to think about and how they needed to approach that thought process. I developed scaffolds that would literally take them through each step of the process even if they had little to no idea how everything would fit together in the end. With these tools, I could have my students up and arguing almost instantly...but that was not necessarily what I wanted. I determined that I wanted my students to fully understand the process and the WHY behind what they were doing in class. So of course, I explained it to them. We toured the individual pieces of arguments and how they fit together to create a winning thought process that could not be defeated by other thinkers. I explained that they had to support every assertion that they made with data and evidence. I helped them to see (in an interesting twist) that they had to reason through everything for their audience. They were responsible for the thinking and their audience should not be thinking for themselves. We toured the different kinds of reasoning and the basic reasoning patterns. Together we determined why fallacies of reasoning would not make their arguments stronger, but instead would invite their audience to think for themselves as they saw the holes in the evidence. Counterpoints and rebuttals were seen as the way to shut the opposition up and allow more time for the focus to be on the arguer. All things came together and they were getting it.

We applied their newfound knowledge and skills to four basic argumentative sessions that first semester and those students truly mastered the content. I am not sure if they could forget it if they tried. We toured the historical arguments behind the development of the science we were studying. We picked out the specific pieces in others' arguments that we were learning to create on our own, all along using the subject matter at hand topically. Students applied the science to current controversial situations in the real world around them and they made adult decisions that would make government officials wonder why they hadn't thought of that. These students worked in small groups to help each other out and they competed in online forums to have the most bulletproof claim and evidence. In the end, through all of the sweat and mental exercise, they learned. They worked harder than they ever thought they could or would and they wanted for extra minutes in science class because there was no way that class could be over yet...it had just started. They worked as teams and they went through the unit together as a learning community.

They worked harder than they ever thought they could or would and they wanted for extra minutes in science class because there was no way that class could be over yet...it had just started.

So what actually happened, specifically? At first I was somewhat lost myself. Even as a researcher and a student of scientific argumentation, understanding how to implement it was a different story. So I went with what I had derived from some experience in a language arts setting and had the students try and break down someone else's argument as they researched a topic searching for background knowledge and understanding of the grand scheme of things. We were just starting a unit on electricity and magnetism, so I though why not examine the historical debates between Edison and Tesla. I quickly realized that I had not done enough research myself, because students had a plethora of questions regarding what was going on with the debate and the specific assertions that were being made by these two thinkers. Even though I knew I had a good understanding of electricity, alternating current, direct current, and the main ideas of these debates, I did not have a thorough enough knowledge of all the events that took place over the course of these debates to answer all of my students' questions. That is when I figured out for the first time how much work this was going to be for me, too. However, I also realized that my students would absolutely have to develop a deep understanding of the material in order to construct any level of real scientific argument. I didn't mind working hard, and they seemed to not mind working hard either. Thinking hard, however, may have been a different story.

At first they really just wanted to copy down information and not really even read it in some cases. Most students spent their time copying and pasting lines from the webpages into the evidence and reasoning parts of the argument scaffold. Sometimes they could not even articulate what the argument was. We did not get off to a great start. As I quizzed them on content, they were still not even sure what AC or DC power was. Ugh. I had to fight my instinct to give direct instruction on the content and trust that my plan would work. So we had small group discussions and peer reviews of the arguments (which the kids really had to read and identify the pieces of according to the scaffold). As students identified that in general the arguments made little to no sense, I asked why they thought that might be the case. As there generally is, one honest and perceptive student (sometimes there is only one) pointed out that she really just skimmed to find something she thought fit in the right box. So we had the first of many discussions about focus and reading for information. We discussed the fact that there was no reason for a word or phrase to not make sense, as they were on a computer connected to the internet. Google, as I often say, is a beautiful thing. Throughout the discussion, though, as a group they seemed to be able to piece together a bit of the understanding of AC/DC current as we worked together to also power through the arguments of Edison and Tesla. I would say the most shocking parts for the students were the fact that Tesla should be far more well-known for his contributions to our modern use of electricity and that Edison electrocuted and elephant. I refused to give direct instruction, though. We would work together or they would have to make another attempt on their own. This time we did it together, after all this was pretty new to all of us.

We moved on to the next step in the general instruction and learned some other pieces of electromagnetism content through other general teaching methods before we arrived at the next scheduled opportunity for argumentation. This event began with some experiential education on series and parallel circuits. After making some craft related representations of the possible way to wire using series and parallel configurations (involving pictures of batteries and bulbs along with string for wire), we experimented with actually wiring batteries, switches, bulbs, and fuses in different configurations. Students were given some paths to follow and other times they just experimented with different kinds of wiring. After working with these and then discussing as a class some of the benefits of each kind of wiring, students were given the situation of wiring Christmas lights and asked to create an argument describing which kind of wiring would be best for the situation. I provided some reading material for them and some general wiring diagrams for differing brands of Christmas lights. I also gave them my "getting your evidence together" and "reasoning scaffolds" to go along with their "creating an argument" scaffold from the previous activity. (Teaching materials can be found in the appendix.) After their poor performance, I knew they needed more help.

They worked in pairs this time. We were still focused solely on the first three steps: claim, evidence, and reasoning. Many students immediately gravitated towards the idea of parallel wiring because some of them had spent time looking for that one bulb that had burned out in a line of lights. There was finally some dissention when they came across the pricing of wiring and the parallel lights compared to the series lights. Overall, the students had pretty well thought out claims and reasoning. However, almost every single argument seemed to substitute their reasoning where there should have been evidence. (This is and has been the bane of my existence when it comes to argumentation.) As I walked around working with students I felt like I said, "why" about a million times. Some folks got it and some did not. Once again I convinced myself that practice was the most important thing and that they did have good ideas about parallel and series wiring. They were getting the content much better this time. I had broken the information down a little more for them to make it easier to digest and we had done an experiment so they had experience. More background knowledge seemed to correlate with better arguments. This was not shocking, as research identified similar results. Students were still using the peer evaluation rubrics to both drive their arguments and to evaluate their peers in their argumentative prowess. Students who were asking themselves the questions on the scaffolds were progressing well. On the weekly quiz, there were few if any misconceptions about wiring. After the Friday quiz we watched a silly Science Court episode about wiring. I had the students pick out the specific evidence that supported the claim in the clip. I made sure to tell them I did not want any reason at all. This helped them focus on facts, facts, and only facts. I still had some reasoning given, but there were many more facts than they had used as evidence in the first two arguments they created. The separation of evidence from reasoning seemed far more difficult for the students than I had anticipated.

To my pleasure, students came in the next day having done independent research at home. SCORE!!!

We were getting to the real nitty gritty of the electromagnetism unit now. Students were grasping the different kinds of current and the wiring configurations. We took some time to diagram the flow of the electrons in the different kinds of wiring as we moved on to static electricity. I wanted them to fully understand the flow of electrons before we talked about the gathering of the electrons and how they discharged. After some demonstrations on static electricity and illustrations of what was happening to the electrons, we moved on to the third argumentative session. For this session, since students had grasped the main concepts through experimentation, argumentation, and good old fashioned tried and true teaching, I crafted an argument that would get them excited, engaged, wondering, and digging deeper into real world science. The topic of our experience was static electricity and gas station fires. For this session, we spent the first day watching the Mythbusters episode "Gas Station Fires Mini-Myth." In this episode they detailed the possibilities of fires and explosions being caused by static electricity, explained how it happens, and experimented to recreate the scenario in which a gas station exploded due to a static spark igniting gasoline fumes. The next day in class students began to discuss the scenario immediately, which I took as a good sign. I provided students with significant reading material detailing everything I could find about the discussion in science trade publications, newspapers, online articles, and current policies regarding gas stations dealing with possible electric discharge fires. We also examined data on instances of these kinds of fires and the amount of fill-ups that happen each day. All in all, students had a plethora of data to sift through as they developed and nurtured their claims. Students worked in groups of three on this occasion, as there was a significant amount of reading and research to be done. To my pleasure, students came in the next day having done independent research at home. SCORE!!!

With everything going better than expected and students proceeding well in their division of data and reasoning, I decided that these groups of three were ready to work on counterarguments and rebuttals. In order to do this, I set up some online chat rooms that students could access anonymously. They were anonymous to each other, but not to me. I had them detail their claim, evidence, and reasoning in the chat rooms and them visit the arguments of three or more other groups to critique their arguments and, if their claim differed, to offer their claim as a counterclaim and provide at least two pieces of evidence to support their counterclaim.   Due to the serious critiques students offered as they rated arguments using my peer argument evaluations, I knew that they would have no mercy in their online critiques, especially since they were anonymous. I was right. They were brutal to each other, but that was a good thing. On the third day, students filled in their "creating an argument" scaffold to detail their argument, counterarguments that were suggested, and the rebuttal that they had planned to negate the counterarguments provided.   Through reading their scaffolds, I could tell that these students had developed a significant understanding of how static electricity worked and they were detailing their ideas for what should or should not be done as far as rules and regulations for gas station fill-ups were concerned. To take it a step further, I had students transfer this argument to essay form.

I am not sure I will ever get kids to love non-fiction writing in the same way that I do, but these students were ready to put their arguments into their own words. They seemed more prepared because they had a true grasp of the material and figured the essay would be one of the easier ones they had written (or so they said to me). What I received is still some of the best argumentative writing I have ever gotten from students. With the developing ideas that they had worked out in their groups and then in their online forum, students proceeded to solidify what they wanted to say, develop reasoning to show causation, and then more reasoning to support whether they thought there should be regulations on pumping gas. This ended up being better than any other arguments that they worked on during the unit. With my experience in writing, I have always found that I state my ideas more succinctly in essay form when I have a clear rubric to follow. Students had the argument mapped

out, then as they wrote, the developed their reasoning more
thoroughly and explained themselves more clearly. They examined
the situation from multiple angles and could support and refute many
sides to the situation. In this writing, they did everything that I had
wanted them to do, and they understood what they were saying. The
best part was that this was enrichment. They had already mastered
the majority of the electricity part of the electromagnetism content
through the experiments, some flipped classroom lectures, and the
first two argumentative sessions.   I took a leap of faith and it paid off.

Form here we moved into the magnetism part of the
electromagnetism unit, which took the students only three days to
really get through, working in the same manner that they had for
electricity. They did some hands on activities with magnets and iron
filings, we discussed them, and they watched a 15 minute lecture
video I had created for them. The magnetism content was short and
relatively simplistic. Essentially it was a survey of the basics
concerning how magnets work and magnetic field lines. We also
discussed generators momentarily. From there we went to the grand
finale of our foray into scientific argumentation. We tackled another
topic that could be classified as socio-scientific in nature. The students
and I spent four full class days examining the issues surrounding
above or below ground high voltage power lines with a concentration
on electromagnetic field (EMF) radiation. I provided students with
another significant helping of pamphlets, regulatory practices, cost
data, health issue research, health issue denial, and many websites to
visit for a grand tour of a subject matter that has two very distinct
sides, both with significant amounts of data and support. This was also
an enrichment unit, and all of my colleagues thought I was crazy for
using such a technical and emotional topic for 8th grade students. I

guess it is a good thing no one in administration had any idea what I was doing, because this subject matter was essentially high school engineering (11th and 12th) grade subject matter and only very loosely related to the standards I was supposed to be getting my kids ready to test on. Whatever...we did it anyway.

The students spent a full two days researching their topic. When they began discovering the associated health issues that proponents of burying lines purported as having a coexistence with the EMF radiation, they were more interested than ever. Many may already know this, but many schools are built very near high voltage power lines due to the lower land prices. It soon became obvious that they saw a direct connection to their lives and the kinds of decision making they would need to make as adults. This material was dense and technical. I was pretty impressed with the way these students went about their business and asked as many questions as they needed in order to understand what they needed to know to work out their arguments. Some of these groups got somewhat heated in their discussions of the costs benefit analyses coupled with the notions of multiple contradictory studies. This was a perfect topic to really focus on the counterarguments and rebuttals because of the many contradictions in thinking, reporting of evidence, and studies in general. I did not require the essay in the end because we only had the four days to work on this argument and the students spent more time actively engaged in the research than I expected. However, I am not one to stop kids who are working hard to learn enrichment materials. They did work in their groups to complete the "constructing an argument" scaffold again and many made use of my "getting your evidence together" and "reasoning scaffolds" to help hash out their ideas and make sure they were complete. I did receive two phone calls from parents who were wondering why their students were so intense in discussing their stance on the subject with their parents. It happened that they were not impressed with living so close to the high voltage power lines. Oh well. You can't win 'em all!

In the end, students came out of this unit with far more advanced knowledge than the other students in the 8th grade who were in the same unit. In only the time of one five week unit on electromagnetism students had learned the basics of argumentation through experience and only a small amount of explicit instruction. These same students had developed an understanding of a new way of thinking and developed confidence in themselves as high level thinkers. When the unit test came around at the end of the five weeks, only the few students who absolutely refused to try and put forth an effort failed to be successful. Most students scored higher than they had ever scored on an exam. What was wonderful was that over half of the students were 90% proficient in the subject matter and 12 students did not miss a single question. Even with all of the mistakes that I made in my first foray into argumentation with my students, I could not have been more proud of their success and the results overall. Since that group of students, I have implemented these processes over and over with middle and high school students in order to develop the process that I think works.

I know I will never forget what happened in that short month in my classroom. Those students still keep in touch with me through various means and at a far higher rate than any other group. I think it was special because it was both of our initiation into argumentation in a science class. We were in the same boat and we all knew it. Although I would like to say I wouldn't change a thing, it is very fortunate for the reader that I decided to change a lot (as you will see in the next chapter). Out of the mouths of those students are many epiphanies that I consider to this day as I apply the concepts of argumentation in my continued work with students. Although I have moved on to teaching high school juniors and seniors, they still approach the concepts with the same wonder and amazement when I introduce them, as they are as completely foreign to them as argumentation was to my middle school students.

There were negative perceptions from time to time, but in general, the students had positive experiences and felt as though they would use the ideas as they moved on to high school and college. It is my most sincere hope that as you work through the rest of this volume and implement the upcoming strategies with your students that you will have the same great outcomes as I have.

What Students Say:

"When you find out the data and facts to support what you are arguing about, the ideas just seem to come together"

"It is tough to try and figure out what the other person is going to say"

"I can find whatever is wrong with my argument and fix it if I think about what I thought and what else could explain or connect to it"

"I understand this stuff so much better now"

"Is this that critical thinking everyone is always talking about?"

"When I relate it to me, I can think about it better"

"Doing the research is most helpful"

"While I was learning the classwork, I was learning how to apply that knowledge to argumentation"

How the Unit was Organized

Monday 3-3: Electricity and Magnetism pre-test. Introduction to argument including the creation of a chart detailing both sides of a debate. 1st and 2nd – apple vs. android. 3rd – evolution vs. creationism. 4th -

Tuesday 3-4: Review the homework video. Began construction of series and parallel circuits using string and pictures.

Wednesday 3-5:

AC vs. DC Argument Assignment:

On the board –

 1: Use the Ac and DC websites to increase your knowledge of both AC and DC currents.

2: Use the rest of the websites, which detail the Edison vs. Tesla arguments to fill out your argument sheet based on Either Edison's or Tesla's argument.

Thursday 3-6:

Reexamine the AC DC debate. Have students work in pairs to discern the debate main points and the benefits and drawbacks of each kind of current. Go over as a class. Watch the goanimate productions created by teacher detailing the debate's main points.

Finish series and parallel representations including directional arrows to show the direction of the power.

Friday 3-7: Quiz to discern what students have ascertained as far as basic premises of circuits and currents. Watch science court episode on electric current. Students write the basic evidence and reasoning used in the Science Court Episode.

Monday: 3-10-14: Paired argument creation with research on series an parallel circuits

Tuesday: 3-11 – Static electricity activity and continue per argument development

Wednesday: 3-12 – Using what was learned from peer argument development activity, write your argument in paragraph form. Then peer review using peer argument review sheet.

Thursday: 3-13 – Read article on Static electricity. Watch Mythbusters segment on static charges and gas station fires. Begin developing argument based on this information by using the full grouping of Scaffold sheets. Producing the data to support an argument

Realized today that the Mythbusters are an excellent example of scientific argumentation

Friday 3-14 – Quiz. Finish argument development. Introduce the full array of argument scaffolds

Monday 3-17: Circuits Lab – Creating different versions of series and parallel circuits

Tuesday 3-18: Finish Arguments on static elec. And gas stations. Online discussion.

Wednesday 3-19: Resistance – Practice Problems

Thursday 3-20: Resistance, Vocabulary review game

Friday 3-21: Quiz – Power Plants

Monday 3-24: Illustrated Dictionary

Tuesday 3-25: Magnets Activity

Wednesday 3-26: Argument Research – Burying High Voltage Power Lines

> Day 1: Research based on issues on both sides of High Voltage Power Lines Issue

Thursday 3-27: Argument–High Voltage Power Lines

Day 2: Students decide on a claim and construct their argument using argument scaffolds.

Friday 3-28: Quiz, Students finish arguments and create their presentations.

Monday 3-31: Induction electricity video and readings/Vocabulary Game

Tuesday 4-1 Study Guide/Presentations of Arguments

Wednesday 4-2: Computer Lab/Research Questions Interview

Thursday 4-3: Review Game

Friday 4-4: Electricity and Magnetism Test/Argument Test

Chapter 5

Putting Argumentation to Work in YOUR Classroom

This section has the complete implementation plan and a snapshot of some materials to use. As you read, think about your curriculum area and how these practices fit.

As you read decide if you need more information or a better understanding of how to implement these practices.

As you read imagine how your students would react to these kinds of experiences.

Think about total implementation as scientific argumentation is something that takes teacher buy in and commitment.

Imagine what your colleagues might say about these methods.

Will you get buy in and support from your colleagues and administration?

Finally, think about your experiences with his manner of thinking.

When I'm getting ready to reason with a man, I spend one-third of my time thinking about myself and what I am going to say -- and two-thirds thinking about him and what he is going to say.

- Abraham Lincoln

Some who write about educational issues, such as Becker (2010) and Scott (2011) focus on the strict policy of the US government requiring scientific and research based proof of efficacy regarding educational practices and thereby the monetary outlay that accompanies those practices when supported by government policy. I feel like part of the answer is to give educators something that works, is scientifically and research based and proven, and that they can manipulate to fit whatever they are doing. It continually builds on itself to make each session a contributor to greater success in the next session, but also overall scholastically.

The theoretical and experiential venture into scientific argumentation that I have tried to detail illuminates (I believe) the fact that this is both scientifically proven and sound, but at the same time, is common-sensical and a natural progression within childhood itself. One of the first questions answered for students, or more aptly by students, within the concept of scientific argumentation is the all-important, "Why?" The question is one which reminds one of their childhood while simultaneously reminding parents of the question that seems to never be answered to a child's satisfaction. I often told them if they continually asked themselves "Why?" and "So what?" that they would get where they were going. For those who choose to implement the conceptual circus that scientific argumentation can be it is most important to know what you are doing. This is not a technique, strategy, or fly-by-night fix for the educational industry. This is the way scientific knowledge has been constructed for as long as history has told tales of the past.

The complicated task of developing consensus scientific understanding, or for that matter consensus understanding in any field, is long and demanding. Using this method in teaching will develop lasting and uncommonly thorough knowledge and understanding. Here, I will attempt to outline a process for teaching and using scientific argumentation in science, language arts, and social science classrooms. The generalized argumentation aspects along with the basic reasoning patterns can be applied to most subject areas, even Math (think proofs). The general differences come along with what is accepted as evidence and expertly derived information.

Claims/Qualifiers:

What is it?

This is your argument.

What are you trying to prove or convince someone of?

Make this statement clear and precise.

This is where you state any qualifying situations in which your claim is or is not true.

Questions to Ask Yourself

What am I trying to prove?

What am I saying is the correct answer or explanation?

What am I saying is the right idea or interpretation?

Is my claim true all of the time?

Is my claim only true in certain situations?

IN THE BEGINNING...there were blank slates that are our students. HAHA we wish. Just as with any concept, it is a good rule of thumb to introduce the topic or concept in some way that gets students interested and wanting more. So:

Step 1: Introduce the idea of a claim

The idea of a claim is not magical in any way. It will often be compared to a thesis statement and to a mere identification of what you support or deny. However, it is a good idea to begin with having students understand that they must be specific and explicit in what they stand for in any situation. Language is important as it is the way in which we communicate our thoughts with others. The language of argument must be specific and descriptive. Simply stated, they must pay attention to what they say. There is no way to oversell the importance of clarity in speech and wording. Clarity of the written word both demonstrates and leads to clarity of thoughts. There have been countless experiences in my own life and in the work of my students where having to communicate ideas through both speech and the written word has led to more precise ideas. The actual act of writing something down involves the communication with self that, if done correctly, develops the best possible work.

Communicating with self is a part of literacy training at all levels. The intra-personal conversations one has are pivotal to complete comprehension. I try to demonstrate these conversations and my thought processes for my students through think alouds. This is a "go to" method for me in teaching most anything. I know that I have been trained to think well and thus I am sure that my experiences will also help my students to learn to think well. I have introduced claims in multiple ways, but one of the easiest with all ages of students is to start asking their opinions about current topics that generally polarize individuals in their age group. I always shy away from topics that are controversial in real life or inappropriate in any way. My favorite is the cell phone debate. Everyone seems to have an opinion about this, whether they have a cell phone or not. So I ask:

Which is the better or best kind of cell phone?

OR

Which is better, Apple or Andriod?

In the most well behaved classrooms, I see hands raised immediately. In most of my classes, though, I hear 30 – 38 voices at once...all with their opinions. This is generally the reaction I have gotten with a well-chosen subject. Peaking their interest is important. Teasing them a bit throughout the experience by telling them that they could soon be the person to convince everyone else of their idea is even better. They do so love to be right. In any case, as we begin to dissect the idea of what they see as their stance on whatever topic we are using, I begin to question students as to the source of their position. This is a handy way to begin the introduction of evidence as well. Claims and data/evidence are difficult to separate sometimes. Reasoning patterns can also begin to appear within these discussions. If you are a believer of holistic learning, then an introductory session can include all parts of the argument. At any rate, it is good to start pinpointing the development of their ideas and the clarification of their claim. I have developed a scaffold to help students construct a claim that can be supported by both data/evidence and reasoning and at the same time gets them thinking about a preliminary counterargument. However, at first I generalize a few questions and ask the students to think about them individually.

1. *What is your stance or position regarding (whatever topic you have chosen)?*

2. *Why have you taken this position?*

3. *Does your position apply all of the time, or is there a possibility that it will change?*

4. *How can you state your position clearly and specifically?*

Another way that I have introduced the idea of the claim in a science specific environment is to create a specific part of a lab or experiment that requires students to identify one scientific idea, theory, or law that they could claim to be true based on their experiment or lab data. I have also created a scientific argumentation based lab write-up that I have used, but I do not introduce that fully until after the pieces of argument have been discussed in class. So after the first lab session of the year, which is usually during the first week of school, I get my students thinking of what they can prove based on the lab results. Real science is based on these kinds of activities, so it serves multiple purposes to introduce this way of thinking from the outset. Students need to consider the claim that can be made based on the actual science involved. This also helps student to get far more out of their lab experiences. I try to choose a lab or experiment that is a bridge between the sciences from their previous year and the current year. If that is not possible, there are plenty of activities that are merely based on the foundations of science that all students need every year.

An example that may be appropriate for multiple grade levels is a basic inquiry lesson involving the easy and quick whirly-bird lab. The basic premise of the lab is using a folded piece of paper that takes advantage of its shape to spin as it falls. The air resistance causes the whirly-bird to slow as it spins and falls. During the lab the students cut the "blades" of the whirly-bird. The shorter wings obviously have less air resistance and thereby fall faster. Students can be asked to assert their explanation of what they experienced during the lab in the form of a claim.

WHIRLEY BIRD LAB

PROBLEM: How does the length of a paper whirly bird's wings affect how long it stays in flight?

GATHER INFORMATION:

Objects all fall to the ground at the same rate because gravity is the same for all objects. An object can be slowed down by what is call **fluid friction** or **air resistance**.

When you drop a piece of paper that is flat and one that is crumpled, which piece of paper will hit the ground first?   If you try this, you'll find that the crumpled paper will get to the ground faster because of what is called **air resistance**, a type of friction.

MATERIALS: stop watch, whirly bird pattern, ruler, and scissors

PROCEDURES:

1. Cut out the patterns for whirly birds. Cut along all **SOLID** lines. Fold along the **dotted** lines in the following manner:
   a. Fold C and D back so they overlap somewhat onto each other.
   b. 'Fold the small tab at the bottom up onto the ends of C and D to keep them folded.
   c. Fold A and B in opposite directions along their dotted lines. This will look a bit like the blades of a helicopter.
2. Choose one student to be the person in charge of dropping the whirly bird from the same height for each trial
3. Choose one person to time how long each whirly bird stays in the air.
4. Drop the whirly bird with the 7 cm wings and time how long it takes to hit the ground. Repeat this step two more times.
5. Then cut 1cm off of each wing.
6. Drop the whirly bird with the 6 cm wings and time how long it takes to hit the ground. Repeat this step two more times.
7. Then cut 1cm off of each wing.
8. Drop the whirly bird with the 5 cm wings and time how long it takes to hit the ground. Repeat this step two more times.
9. Find the average of each whirly bird by adding up the three trials and dividing the sum by 3.
10. Graph the averages

Flight Time of Whirly Birds

Whirly Bird Wing Lengths	Trial 1 Time in seconds	Trial 2 Time in seconds	Trial 3 Time in seconds	Average
7cm				
6cm				
5cm				

CONCLUSIONS

Which whirly bird stayed in flight the longest?_____

Which whirly bird stayed in flight the shortest?_____

What was your hypothesis? Explain whether you were correct or not.

Which whirly bird experienced more air resistance or fluid friction?

What other patterns do you see in your data chart?

How would this be different on the moon?
What effect would adding weights o the whirly bird have on its falling? Why?

Scientific Argumentation-Based Lab Debrief

As you approach any laboratory activity, you should focus on what you can learn about the physics involved through the activity. Activities are performed in physics class for the purpose of inquiring about the scientific laws and theories we are learning. As such, this should be the directions your attention goes.

You will construct a scientific argument based on the lab activity performed. Remember that a scientific argument used specific

Claim: Looking at what you did in the lab, what we are studying in class, and what the data show, you can develop an idea or some understandings that you can show to be true.

Claim:

_____

_____

_____

_____

_____

_____

_____

Notes:

In a mathematic based setting, I have also worked with students to identify the math rules that they could claim to be true with regards to how they solved the problem they are working on. This is appropriate at many age groups. Through the act of examining how a math problem is solved and how the answer is checked for accuracy, one can discern some of the mathematical laws or common practices that have gone into the solving of the problems. The goal is to have the students think of something that they can claim to be true based on the problem at hand.

A good way to use math to introduce claims is examining the order of operations. The concept itself is important at all levels of mathematics and is relatable to enough lessons that essentially anyone can use it anytime. Using any problem that the order of the operations is important, students can be questioned as to what mathematical law or concept they could assert as true based on what they have done in their problem. Essentially, students are stating their claim as to the method of solving a problem or stating the claim as to what they are proving. This is merely an introduction, the concepts of argumentation can be used throughout mathematics to help students understand why they should show their work and also to get them to see math in a more productive way.

With math using argument is also a viable option for making assertions for how to solve word problems. The use of the logic involved and having students make claims as to what they are thinking and then following that up with evidence and the progression through the actual solutions is perfect for using argumentation in mathematics.

What assertion or claim can you make about the methodology to use to solve the following word problem?

You have the option of joining a music download service with one of three plans. Determine which plan is best for a 3 month membership in which you download 100 songs.

Plan 1:$4.99 per month and 2 cents per song

Plan 2:$5.99 per month sand 1.2 cents per song

Plan 3: $8.88 per month and unlimited songs

You can make a claim asserting that Plan 3 is better mathematically if you solve for the total cost of each plan, number 3 has the lowest cost even though it has a lover monthly fee.

The complete page of reasoning and proof could look like the following:

Stating a Claim in Math

What can you state about the following problems that you can prove mathematically?

2x3+5 -1=?

Here you can state the claim that the proper way to solve this problem involves following the accepted rules of mathematics involving the order of operations.

In order to solve the equation, multiply 2 and 3 together. Then add 5. Complete the equation by subtracting 1.

2x+10=18

Here you can follow the basic rules of algebra to provide a claim as to the proper methodology and the proper answer.

To solve for x it is necessary to follow the rules of reverse operations to isolate the x variable. First, subtract 10 from both sides of the equation because the 10 is being added to the left side. This will leave 2x=8. Then follow this by dividing both sides of the equation by 2, because the 2 is multiplied by the x. This leaves x=4.

In language arts class I have used the idea of claims based on the interpretation of literature. Once again, this is something that I introduce early in the year, so I simply look for any place in which interpreting texts is applicable. The claim itself is the reader's view of what has been read. There are multiple places in the common core standards which call for students to read, interpret, and support their interpretations with textual evidence. Defining the claim is one of the pieces to interpreting text, and students should be sure that they are clear and precise when they do so. A part of learning to state a claim is to make sure that it is clear, says exactly what the reader is thinking, and at the same time can be supported.

Poetry is a very good place to start a lesson on defining a clear and precise claim. When reading such works as "Nothing Gold can Stay" by Robert Frost, one can examine the extended metaphor as their claim. "I Know Why the Caged Bird Sings" is also a very good poem to elicit specific insights and a personal connection from students. A part of the focus should be to make sure that the claim can be sustained and supported. This should allow for multiple different claims, as do many works of poetry. To be more "21st Century" song lyrics can be examined in the same way. Overall, symbolism and especially extended metaphors are nice to begin with because they offer a wide variety of claims.

Nothing Gold Can Stay

Robert Frost, 1874 - 1963

Nature's first green is gold,

Her hardest hue to hold.

Her early leaf's a flower;

But only so an hour.

Then leaf subsides to leaf.

So Eden sank to grief,

So dawn goes down to day.

Nothing gold can stay.

When considering an interpretation of Robert Frost's poem "Nothing Gold Can Stay" closely examine the following:

What might the author be saying through metaphor, simile, allusion, and other literary device?

Is there anything about the author's life that might contribute to the meaning of the poem?

What was happening during the time period that the poem was written which may contribute to the intended meaning of the poem?

What do the words and the way in which they are written mean to you?

How can you meld what the author may have intended with what you perceive into your interpretation?

In a social studies class, the interpretation of evidence is very important to getting students interested and involved. Social studies as discipline, at its heart, is the interpretation of primary documents and evidence that we have uncovered or experienced in the past. Examining diaries and first person accounts of historic events give time periods, and the mindset of people within those times, a different flavor and can serve well to bring them to life. I use as much first-hand experience as possible when I work with students in social studies. I also take care to allow them to have their own opinions and discussions before I offer my personal interpretation. Most often, I still use the think aloud as a primary tool for exhibiting the kind of thinking and mental exercises that would be useful for students as they tackle such critical thinking.

An experience that I have used with both middle school aged students and high school students revolves around the Boston Massacre. After introducing the topic of the happenings of March 5, 1770, I provide the students with two readings. One is from the point of view of a shop keeper who witnessed the happenings first-hand. The other is from a high ranking military officer. Students read both accounts and then they are tasked with one of two chores: 1) sometimes I have them merely choose the story that they believe to be true or 2) I have them create a version of the story that they deem accurate based on the information that they have in the two accounts. Either of these could be formulated as a claim and this allows for social studies students to create a claim and make sure, once again, that it is clear, precise, and states exactly what the student wants it to say. It is important to make sure that the claim leaves no room for interpretation. It must be well-defined and specific enough that way. This particular exercise is also good for introducing claim and evidence at the same time, if the teacher so chooses.

Two Accounts of the Boston Massacre

I.   **John Tudor, a Boston merchant was an eyewitness to the events of March 5, 1770. He wrote:**

On Monday evening the 5th, a few minutes after nine o'clock, a most horrid murder was committed at the courthouse door by eight or nine soldiers under the command of Captain Thomas Preston.

This unhappy affair began when some boys and young fellows threw snowballs at the sentry placed at the courthouse door. At this, eight or nine soldiers came to his aid. Soon after, a number of people collected. The Captain commanded the soldiers to fire, which they did, and three men were killed on the spot and several mortally wounded, one of which died the next morning.   The captain soon drew off his soldiers up to the main guard; if he had not done this, the result might have been terrible, for when the guns fired, the people were alarmed and set the bells a-ringing as if for a fire, which drew many to the place of action.

Lt. Governor Hutchinson which was commander-in-chief was sent for and came to the council Chamber, where some of the judges waited. The Governor desired the crowd to separate about ten o'clock and go home peaceably. He said he would do all in his power to see that justice was done. The 29th Regiment was then under arms on the south side of the Townhouse, but the people insisted that the soldiers should be ordered to their barracks before they would separate. When this was done, the people separated at about on o'clock.

Captain Preston was arrested by a warrant given to the high sheriff by the Justices Dana and Tudor. He was questioned at about two o'clock, and we sent him to jail soon after three, having enough evidence to commit him, because he ordered the soldiers to fire; so about four o'clock the town became quiet. The next day the eight soldiers that fired on the inhabitants were sent to jail.

II.   *General Gage, a British General, wrote the following to a friend in England, five days after the incident:*

On the evening of March 5th, the people of Boston had a great uprising. They began by attacking several soldiers in a small street, near the barracks of the 29th Regiment. The noise of the attack caused several officers to come out of the barracks and investigate. They found some of the soldiers greatly hurt, but they took the soldiers into the barracks.

The mob followed them to the barracks door, threatening and waiving clubs over the officer's heads. The officers tried to make peace, and asked the mob to leave.

Part of the mob then broke into a meetinghouse, and rang the bell as if there were a fire. This seems to have been a prearranged signal. Immediately many people assembled in the streets. Some of them were armed with guns, but most carried clubs and similar weapons.

Many people came out of their houses, thinking there was a fire. Several soldiers, thinking there was a fire, headed to their duty posts as they were supposed to do. On the way they were insulted and attacked. Those who could not escape were knocked down and treated very badly.

Different mobs moved through the streets, passing the different barracks. These mobs tried to make the soldiers angry and urged them to come outside. One group went to the main guard and tried to stir up trouble, but they failed. The guard soldiers stood their positions quietly.

From there the mob moved to the customhouses, and attacked a single soldier on guard there. He defended himself as well as he could, and called for help. Several people ran to the main guard to tell of the danger to the soldier.

Captain Preston, who was in charge of the guard that day, was at the main guard station. When he heard of the attack on the soldier, he sent a sergeant and 12 men to aid him. The Captain soon followed to help prevent the troops from starting unnecessary trouble.

The mob attacked the group of soldiers. Some of the mob threw bricks, stones, pieces of ice, and snowballs at the soldiers. Others moved up to the soldiers' bayonets, trying to use their clubs. People in the mob called out to the soldiers to fire their guns, and used insulting language.

Captain Preston stood between the soldiers and the mob and tried to make peace by talking to them, asking them to leave. Some of the mob asked if he intended to order the soldiers to shoot at them. He answered, "Of course not. I am between you and the troops."

His words had no effect. Once of the soldiers, receiving a violent blow, fired his gun. Captain Preston turned around to see *who had fired. He received a blow that was aimed at his head but missed and hit his arm.*

The mob did not see any damage done by the first shot, so they supposed that the soldiers had loaded only with powder and no shot to scare them. They grew bolder and attacked the soldiers with more force, continually striking the soldiers, throwing objects at them, and daring them to fire. The soldiers soon saw that their lives were in danger, and hearing the word "fire" all around them, three or four fired one after another. These shots were followed by three more in the same hurry and confusion. Four or five persons were unfortunately killed, and several wounded.

Captain Preston and the soldiers were soon afterward delivered into the hands of the judges, who committed them to prison.

Using the two accounts of the Boston Massacre, draw and fill in a Venn Diagram as best you can:

Once students have worked to develop their capacity to create claims which are specific and concise, it is time to practice, practice, and practice. I have multiple processes for developing argumentation in students. Some last multiple years, such as the three year middle school rollout; and others are for the typical one year class experience.

Here I will detail the speed and dynamics for the typical one year class. In that case, it is important to weave the idea of the specific language of the claim into every lesson you do. It should become a natural way of thinking for the students, as it will pave the way for everything else they will do as far as argumentation is concerned. It is pivotal for students to understand that they should not really settle on something that they do not think they can prove. The focus should be on the language and specificity, though.

Constructing a Claim

What ideas or position on the subject matter at hand have you developed? What position or idea will you be arguing in favor of or against?

What are the conditions that your claim is true in? Are there times that your claim is not true or reasonable? Write down any situational or case specific requirements of your claim here. (This is uncommon)

Can your claim be supported by evidence, data, examples and fact or theory in the field? If so list a few examples.

Are there other claims that can also be made that are similar to yours? Are there claims that are different than yours? What are they?

How can you state your claim so that it is very clear and precise? Will people reading or listening to your claim be very clear about what you are saying? Have you been specific? Write your Claim as specific and precise as possible here. Be sure to use field appropriate language and vocabulary.

Data and Evidence

What is it?

This is the data that you are using to support your claim.

This can also be referred to as the evidence that you have to show that your claim is correct or the right idea to consider

Questions to Ask Yourself

What facts did I consider when deciding on my claim?

What evidence will convince others that I am right?

What facts/evidence supports my claim?

STEP 2: Supporting the Claim with Data and Evidence

When students have grasped the concept of specificity and completeness of a claim, it is time to move on to data and evidence. Again, as we look at these processes, it will become obvious that claims and data/evidence can easily go together. For more advanced students, that could easily be the case. Much depends on the age group and level of student you are working with. Alas, as we enter the idea of data and evidence, this is where the epistemological beliefs of your discipline come into play. It is pivotal to detail specifically what can be used and referred to as evidence for your discipline. In the introductory period, the idea of evidence to support your statements and claims is important, but as you delve deeper, you should specifically examine what sources constitute legitimate data and evidence.

As the idea of evidence becomes important, the question of

"Why?" arises as fundamental. When a claim is made, there must be something to support that claim. That something is evidence. I often use the term evidence to describe both specific data and evidence in general. For this introduction, I generally use something I call a detailed reading. It is a good way to simultaneously begin the sustained use of literacy skills - specifically reading for information. I also use detailed readings as introductions to most units as opposed to vocabulary or other means of introducing a new unit. The act of searching for ideas that the students are unfamiliar with is important practice for reading skills and for identifying specific support for the claims that I make in the detailed reading. Essentially, a detailed reading is a set of statements that come almost directly from a text. I often use their textbook when possible, because I generally bring in field literature to use in class when teaching and reinforcing content knowledge. I try to make sure the statements are generalized, yet easy to find, because this is an introduction and it should not last more than 35-45 minutes. As students progressively get better with their reading comprehension and the search for evidence, I make these more labor intensive.

Detailed Reading: Intro to Primary Producers 379-402

For each of the following statements, decide whether you agree or disagree. In 1-2 sentences, describe why you feel the way you do. Try and give real world examples from what you have experienced in your life or from what you have learned in previous years to explain your feelings.

Next, you will read the sections in the textbook and do 1 of 2 things:
1. If the statement was true, write the sentence or sentences that provide the proof that the statement is true and give an example.

<u>*Or*</u>

2. If the statement was false, rewrite the statement to make it true <u>and</u> give an example.

Part I.
1. Phytoplankton are important contributors to the food chain, as they are primary producers.
_____ *Agree*   _____ *Disagree*

Why?

Statement was True – Here is the Evidence:	Statement was false- Should be stated as this:

2. Diatoms are highly efficient at photosynthesis.
_____ *Agree*   _____ *Disagree*

Why?

Statement was True – Here is the Evidence:	Statement was false- Should be stated as this:

The general idea is that some of the statements in the detailed readings are true and some of them are false. Once again, these statements represent a claim. Students dig into the text and determine the validity of the statements. Once they have determined whether the statements are true or false, they perform one of two tasks. If the statement is true, they find two pieces of data/evidence to support the fact that the statement is true. If the statement is false, the students rewrite the statement to make it true and then find one piece of evidence in support. I always tell the students to make sure that they find the evidence they plan to use in support before they settle on the validity of the statement (claim). This also helps them in the future to make sure that they have evidence in support of their own claims before finalizing them. The connection between evidence and a claim cannot be underestimated. Without evidence there can really be no claim. This is a good time to explain these concepts in detail to students. Claims without evidence are merely opinions and are unsubstantiated.

In order to develop these skills more completely, as often as possible when students answer questions in class I require them to describe the evidence. Not only does this help to solidify their understandings of the importance of data/evidence in the world, but at the same time allows them to consistently see the connections within the content that they are working with. A more consistent exposure to this kind of thinking makes it come more easily for students and limits uneducated guessing. I encourage educated guesses when appropriate, as they have some evidence in their support and allow students to take what they know and understand and apply it to new situations without fear of "getting it wrong." After all, if the students are not struggling with the information, then someone is not working

hard enough. It could be the teacher or it could be the student.
Overall, having students support their answers to questions
automatically allows them to answer overarching questions of why,
how do you know, why do you think that, etc. They are training their
thinking to examine facts and specifics to influence and drive their
thinking.

In math classroom, this may look as simple as showing the
computations done to get an answer or showing the checking of that
work. However, as math gets more advanced, this could include
mathematical theory. Data and evidence is more of a broad category
that overlaps with the reasoning category for math. Specifically, the
data/evidence used to support the asserted solution are the math rules
and theories that support the asserted solution's methodology.   The
addition of logic games and puzzles can help students to understand
the need for evidence as they make their decisions. In many math
and logic puzzles, students need to look ahead and prepare possible
outcomes. This can be evidence in their decisions to make certain
moves or to use certain numbers. A good example might be Sudoku
puzzles. That need for evidence is a focus that should last for a
significant amount of time before attempting to move on. This lends
itself to a basic tenant of math reasoning and thinking, which is the
need for evidence in the decision making process.

Data and Evidence

*You have the option of joining a music
download service with one of three
plans. Determine which plan is best*

for a 3 month membership in which you download 100 songs.

Plan 1:$4.99 per month and 20 cents per song

Plan 2:$5.99 per month sand 15 cents per song

Plan 3: $8.88 per month and unlimited songs

You can make a claim asserting that Plan 1 is better mathematically.

To provide evidence for your choice, it is necessary to show the mathematical theory that is involved with your thinking regarding how to substitute in 100 downloads into each situation and determine a final cost.

In order to determine the solution to Plan 1, mathematical theory and the property of multiplication states that 20 cents per song multiplied by the 100 songs gives a song cost of 2000 cents, or $20. Using the property of multiplication again, the $4.99 monthly fee for 3 months times a cost of $14.97. Using the property of addition, the monthly fee plus the song fee gives a total cost for plan 1 of $34.97.

In order to determine the solution to Plan 2, mathematical theory and the property of ,multiplication states that 12 cents per song *multiplied by the 100 songs gives a song cost of 120 cents, or $15. Using the property of multiplication again, the $5.99 monthly fee for 3 months times a cost of $17.97. Using the property of addition, the monthly fee plus the song fee gives a total cost for plan 1 of $32.97.*

For plan 3, the property of multiplication shows that $8.88 multiplied by 3 moths give a total cost of $26.64

In Language arts classes, the evidence that students are looking for is not only held in the words of the author, but also in the environment, life experiences, and thought processes of the author. It is true that often times in class teachers have students use the words of the author as support for their interpretations. However, this can be broadened to include biographical information, time period specific information, general genre definitions and processes, and multiple other kinds of influential data. The acceptable evidence for the language arts field is based on the beliefs of those in the fields and this idea should be related to the students at this time. As we try to teach students to think and use data/evidence to drive their thinking, it is pivotal for students to have all of the avenues to pursue evidence that they can. As students attempt to internalize this information and then transfer it to the real world, the multiple places to pursue evidence are important for them to take with them. In cases of interpretation (and most others) it is never a good idea to get all of your evidence from the same place, or even from multiple like-minded places. The interpretation of literary works can be a time where students broaden

their evidentiary horizons. As they work with different pieces of
literature, they can examine multiple avenues to learn about the
background of the author, time period, social standings, and just about
anything that could have had an influence on the production of a piece
as they try to determine what the piece meant to the author and what
it means to them.

*In Robert Frost' Poem Nothing Gold Can Stay, what
evidence can you provide to support your claim or assertions as
to the meaning of the poem?*

Your Claim:

Evidence:

From the Text Itself

Biographical Information about the author

Literary Device

Information from the Literary movement from which the text comes from

Evidence relating to the time period in which the poem was written

In the realm of social studies, similar ideas can come into play. When interpreting what has happened in history it is a necessity to examine the ideologies of the time period, the purpose of the primary source being used, the biographical information of the participants and all other mitigating factors and circumstances. Within social studies it is very important to think critically when examining the evidence in support of a claim. Key analytical positions can examine motivations of participants as well as their status in society and history as a whole. There are countless occasions throughout world history in which groups of people, individuals, and entire populations have their voices silenced when history is told and the "facts" are interpreted. One should always look for the voices not heard and the inspirations of the voices which are. Often, I tell my students to follow the money. So in addition to the general evidentiary bases from language arts, there are also a strong set of new foci for students to use in support of their interpretations, and of course they use them to develop their ideas and claims as well. As in the development of these skills, this should be a long term focus for teaching and learning, thus this is not a one or two lesson idea. The necessity of interweaving the claim and evidence relationship throughout courses and classroom interactions cannot be overstated. These thought patterns must be practiced to make them more efficient for students. Students should be metacognitively aware of the different viewpoints they should be working their way through. It is the awareness that multiple viewpoints must be taken into account that helps students develop the critical thinking skills and the motivations to use them.

In your examination of the Boston Massacre accounts, what evidence can you cite to support your claim or assertion about what actually happened during the event in question?

Your Claim:

Evidence in support of your Claim:

Evidence directly from the text

Evidence regarding the Time Period in History

Evidence regarding the nature pf the situation

Evidence regarding the personal situation of the sources

In the science classroom we find the origination and basis for scientific argumentation. With the idea of evidence in science comes a focus on the epistemological beliefs involved in the realm of science. The understanding that knowledge and science law are constructed through the actual argumentative process is pivotal to science learning. Multiple years and approaches of different scientists, the vetting by other scientists, observation, testing against explaining events from the past, and predicting events still to come is how science knowledge is developed. With these things in mind, students should learn that scientific evidence consists of things such observational data, scientific theory or Law, scientific understanding from scientific experts in their field, scientific journals or literature, and from the experiences of those in scientific endeavors who approach those undertakings with a scientific frame of reference. Cases can be made for the inclusion of other evidence as acceptable depending on the situation, but in general, these are the accepted references for scientists who work in the field, and should thus be the same for those studying and practicing science in the classroom. Once the introduction of the idea of evidence and its connection to the claim is made, I have taken the detailed reading activity a step further and had students put their evidence on sticky notes and then put those notes on chart paper, or the like, that has the original claim statements written on it. Then they can do a gallery walk in which they see what everyone else has used for evidence. As they go around, they can rate the level of evidence used. This serves multiple purposes. First, it allows the students to be mobile rather than sitting in the same spot for the entire class. Also, it allows students to see what others have written and silently compare their position with that of others. As we move into more complex thinking, examining the thinking of others will become increasingly important as students begin to examine things from multiple points of view. A good base of understanding in the realm of what is possible in the minds of others allows for the framework of critical thinking. Also, this allows students to begin the critique of others' work and ideas. The critique here of others' ideas will also lay the groundwork for critical assessment of situations, but also of the counterargument and rebuttal pieces of the argument puzzle.

Once again, with more advanced students, the ideas of claim and evidence can be introduced together. As they are advancing through high school, many should have already developed some understanding of the argumentative essay and the burden of proof therein. As such, simply incorporating these ideas in to the normal function and speech of a class from the beginning of the year can change the dynamics of the way students think and approach their work. One thing that may become obvious to students at this point or after the reasoning process is the fact that it may be necessary to go back and adjust the claim once sufficient evidence is found. Although there should be research or observation that goes into constructing the claim, further research is always necessary to develop the most potent arguments. Therefore, as student do further research and bolster their knowledge of a topic or concept, they may see that their original ideas were not appropriate and that their assertions need to be altered. When this realization strikes some students within the group, it is a good time to reveal (or allow students to work this out during discussion) that the act of argumentation is an iterative concept and that they will more often than not need to go back and forth through the process. I call this journeying along the continuum of argumentation. With my students, I have had many discussions about this journey. I find very often that there are groans when students find out that they are not done thinking at any part along the way. However, once these practices become habits, students begin to desire the truth and the full story that at so many times in life is hidden from us.

Also at this point, depending on what realizations students are making about the nature of looking for suitable evidence and the continuum of argumentation, this may be a good time to explicitly explain the concepts of critical thinking and metacognitive thinking. As a teaching professional, it is a choice that must be made through knowing the students and their abilities. Each class is different and some are more ready to delve into the more dense thinking that comes with the critical assessment of the evidence and reasoning. I have introduced the concepts with the idea of the legitimacy of evidence and sometimes I introduce critical assessment after the students have practiced reasoning. In this volume, I have placed critical thinking and metacognitive thinking after reasoning for the sake of structure.

As I was writing this, I had the opportunity to venture out for a meeting with a colleague who had been excited to try my methods in his own middle school classroom. He was hesitant, as he was in a low SES area with students who generally did not perform well on standardized tests or in the classroom. However, as I told him of the experiences that I had, he was happy to give it a try. It seemed he would rather try the ideas of a friend and colleague than those of people who spend their lives in the world of theory and out of the world of practice. I try to ramble through both simultaneously (with the split personality my students say I have). I digress. He was pleasantly surprised with the way students, who while in other classes could not or would not analyze things without teacher prodding and doing a significant amount of work for them, had developed the habit of supplying proof for the answers they gave to almost any question. Whether it be a simple bell work assignment, questions from the text, oral practice during a lecture, independent thinking questions, or even critical thinking questions, his students were consistently thinking about the why and how of science when they formulated answers.

In their minds, they were requiring proof. When students are realizing that the evidence serves a purpose and is necessary to support their claim, they are ready to begin recognizing the internal conversations that they are having in determining the completeness and appropriateness of their evidence. This is a great time to introduce explicitly the idea of metacognitive thinking. Students who struggle with reasoning understand that they there is a back and forth conversation that one has with a text as they are reading. It is not effective to approach a text and just read through the words. Text comes to life if there is a give and take along with some cognitive influence from the reader to the text. The same can be said for argumentative thinking. Students should be consistently asking themselves if their evidence is legitimate, if their evidence is appropriate for their audience and for their content area, if their evidence supports their claim and most importantly, is there enough evidence to support the claim fully.

As my colleague's students were requiring evidence of themselves, it seems that they were requiring proof of him when he lectured a well, causing him to do a little more research in his preparations. He seemed to shrug it off as the price he paid for quality results. This was about halfway through his school year, and he was just getting ready to introduce reasoning patterns and their connection to evidence and claims (perhaps that is why he wanted to meet for a bite). Either way, it illustrates the point that introducing these concepts early and making them an integral part of the thinking students must do to meet teacher expectations makes each step along the way after much easier. So as he was ready to do, and so are we, let's move on.

Getting Your Evidence Together

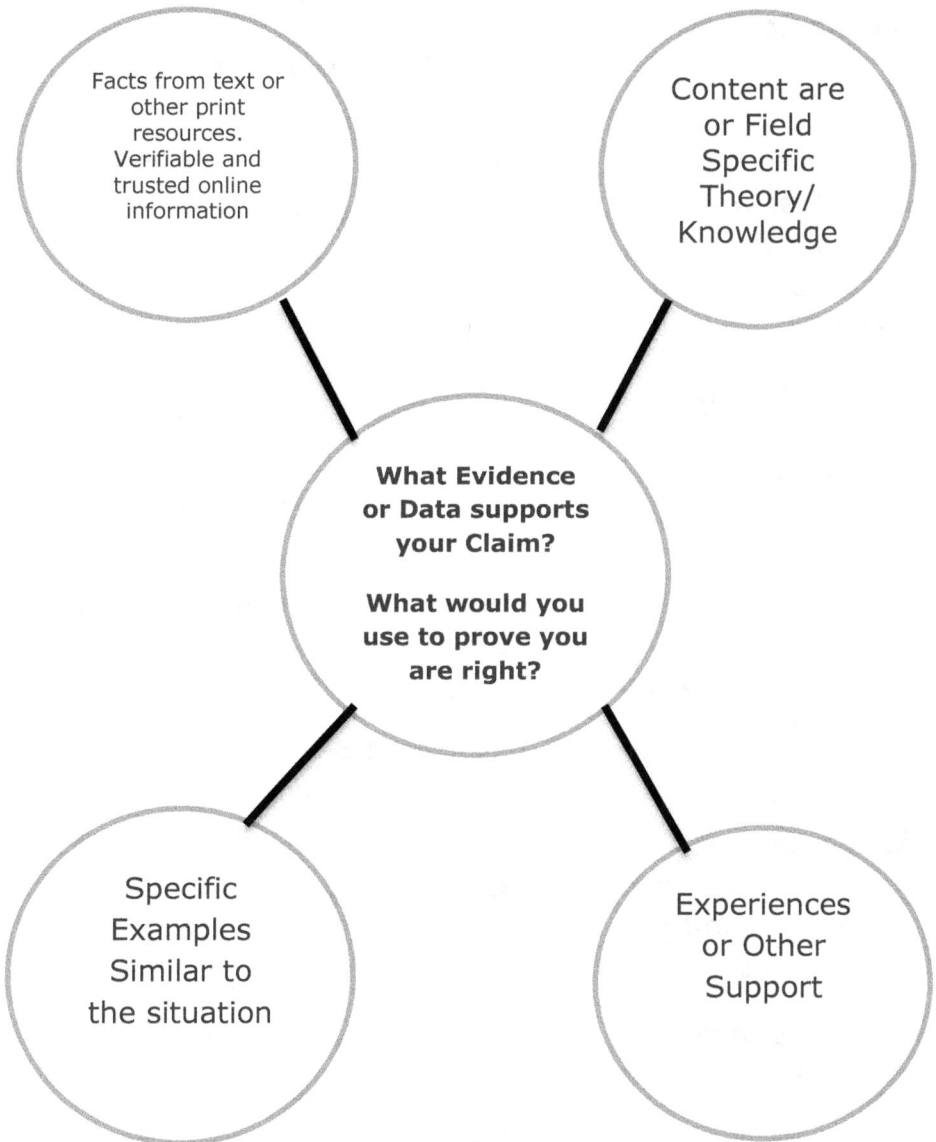

Facts from text or other print resources. Verifiable and trusted online information

Content are or Field Specific Theory/ Knowledge

What Evidence or Data supports your Claim?

What would you use to prove you are right?

Specific Examples Similar to the situation

Experiences or Other Support

Legitimacy:

What it is:

This is where you prove that your evidence should be trusted and is authentic.

You must show your data/evidence to be from legitimate sources and factually based.

Questions to Ask Yourself:

Why is this data/evidence assuredly facts that can be used in this specific field?

Are my sources experts?

Are my sources and facts accepted in the field I am examining?

STEP 2.5: Legitimacy

The idea of legitimacy goes hand in hand with the concept of data and evidence. The data and evidence that is used to support a claim must meet certain requirements to be appropriate. These requirements begin with the basic premise that data and evidence are indeed facts. That applies across the board for anything used to support claims in scientific argumentation. This is one of the specific items that sets scientific argumentation apart from debate and other forms of argument. Although facts may be used to make an emotional appeal in a scientific argument, there is no room for sensationalized opinion or scare-tactics. The social or emotional appeals that can be made in order to confuse or confound in other methods do not apply here. We deal with facts, expert opinions, and supported verifiable observation. Examining evidence and its usefulness involves critical thinking and critically assessing the evidence up close. Students must focus on determining if the evidence is useful and based in fact. Although critical thinking and critical assessment of evidence can be introduced here, I place the full scale study of critical thinking after the introduction of reasoning later in this chapter. As always, this is a decision to be made by the teaching professional as they have the best understanding of where the students are and what they are ready for. The evidence must also adhere to the basis of data and evidence within the specific field or content area of the subject matter at hand.

The work with students and legitimacy is a perfect time to communicate the specific epistemology and requirements for knowledge and understanding in the content area or field that they are arguing in. It is important for students to understand the stance in their content area with regard to what is held as knowledge. If students understand the basic epistemological beliefs for the field they are studying, then they will approach their learning more as their own knowledge construction in the same manner as those in the field. This understanding for students may aid them as they approach new learning. With a basic comprehension and mindset that places them within the field that the content area resides in, students can see themselves outside of the school building and in the real world. Perhaps with this mindset during their approach to their argument, students will see this more as true inquiry and real world interaction rather than another regular assignment. Students can see that the argumentative way of thinking is what happens and how people in the field think and approach their work.

Examine the Legitimacy of your Sources by determining if the source is in a position to be an appropriate source of information or evidence.

Can the evidence be verified?

Can the evidence be corroborated from other sources?

Is the source in a position to know or understand the situation?

Is the source an expert in the field?

Does this source qualify as a source based on the field of study you are in?

Reasoning

What it is:

This is where you show why your data/evidence supports your claim.

You are making the connections and showing why the evidence supports your thinking.

You are also citing field theory or concepts that prove that your evidence does indeed back up your claim.

Questions to Ask Yourself:

Why does my evidence support my claim?

What is the connection between my evidence and my claim?

Why should your evidence be believed as support for your claim?

What scientific theory supports the connections that I have made between my evidence and my claim?

STEP 3: Instruction in Reasoning

Looking forward to the idea of the reasoning that clearly connects the data/evidence to the claim, it is important to note that this is a category that has been forwarded by researchers in the field of argumentation. The reasoning to which I refer is actually directly connected to the concepts of warrants and backing in the Toulmin argument scheme. For Toulmin, warrants and backing are the ideas that encompass the legitimacy of the data/evidence as well as the support that they give the claim. Specifically, warrants show how the data can lead to the claim and backing to the warrants that show why they are legitimate. Currently many practitioners in the field, and also in my research and early teaching practices, warrants and backing have been collapsed into one grand category referred to as reasoning. This is quite simple to do when the epistemological beliefs of the field in which argument is used as a tool are explained in connection with the sources of data/evidence in that area.

If the appropriate and accepted sources are used, then most often the source of evidence will be legitimate. That leaves the connection of the evidence to the claim. All of this can be detailed and worked through by using some common reasoning patterns.

The concepts of reasoning and its connection to data and evidence is something that students tend to confuse from the start. Many of my students, and the colleagues of mine who have tried these practices, notice immediately that students attempt to supply reasoning in place of their evidence. This is why explicit teaching of these concepts is also very helpful. Research (including my own) has shown that students develop a more thorough and complete understanding of scientific argumentation if they have explicit instruction in the structure of argument and reasoning patterns. I breach the topic with a thorough examination of how scientists work to explain themselves fully and to a point where their audience understands and agrees with their line of reasoning or logic. I generally say that in order to win an argument or convince another person of your opinion, it is helpful to do all of the thinking for them. With that juicy bit of information, I lead them to some tried and true reasoning patterns that are effective and follow logical means to an end. I also explicitly explain some fallacies of reasoning that they should avoid. I first explain deductive and inductive reasoning in a basic form:

- Deductive reasoning often has a very clear path. It is often obvious and logical.

  - All mammals are warm-blooded

  - Humans are mammals

- Humans must be warm blooded

- Inductive Reasoning involves drawing conclusions and making some assumptions

    - It is February 14th

    - A man is buying flowers and chocolates

    - The man is buying Valentine's gifts for his significant other.

- You are making observations or collecting data.

- You have many details

- You use these details to develop a theory or generalized statement which applies to more situations than just your current situations

- You go from specific details to a generalization

This is a simplified approach to the basics, but most often, students have not been introduced to reasoning in a formal lesson or in explicit teaching. With that in mind, I prefer to introduce specific reasoning patterns and give some examples. The basic reasoning patterns I start with look like this:

Some Common Reasoning Patterns

- Argument from Analogy

    - Identify something to which what you are arguing clearly applies or is already linked to.

- Then show enough similarities between what you
  are arguing and that other thing to convince
  someone that your idea should apply as well

Analogies are something that people use often in order to help them understand and make sense of the world around them. For instance, in school we often speak of "activating background knowledge" because if you understand a part of something or something that is similar to what you are trying to understand, you can make connections of similarities between two things and this helps to understand the new content more efficiently.   With that in mind, arguing from analogy may look something like this:

Students who have struggled in math in the past and now take a math strategies class in addition to their regular math class report that they are more comfortable in their regular math class and have greater confidence when learning new math concepts. Therefore, students who struggle in science should take a scientific thinking strategies class in addition to their science classes because this may help them in the same way that the math strategies class helped students struggling in math.

- Argument from an Established Rule

  - Showing that there is already a rule or
    established practice that relates to what you are
    arguing.

  - In this case you must show that the established
    rule does indeed apply to what you are arguing.
    You must make the connection

This is also a basic argument that people tend to use in their daily lives. An argument from an established rule may look like the following:

A student comes to class late and is sent to the tardy desk for a pass. The student argues that they should not be sent to the tardy desk because they were only late by 20 seconds or so and they are a good student. The teacher replies that the rule for tardiness is that if a student is not in the classroom when the bell has finished ringing, then they are tardy. This policy was detailed at the beginning of the semester and has been the policy without fail. It would not be fair to allow the student into class without a tardy pass from the tardy desk because this is an established rule that all are aware of.

- Argument from Precedent

    - There is an existing rule or way of doing things that is already accepted

    - You must find the existing rule, or precedent, and point it out along with the connection to what you are arguing

The argument from precedent is pervasive in the American legal system. Judges often make their rulings based on precedent that has been laid down by their predecessors and lawyers argue their cases by using precedent in support of their positions. Argument from precedent is often used in response to an argument from established rule, either showing an exception or showing that the rule does not apply through another instance. This argument scheme is similar in many ways to argument from analogy, but arguing from precedent is usually based on a specific case (as in law), while arguing from analogy is more broadly defined. An example of arguing from precedent might continue the established rule example from before:

In response to the teacher's argument from the established tardy rule and the fact that it is well known and has been explained since the beginning of the semester, the student may argue that another student was allowed in tardy on a specified occasion, "You let Jose in last week on Tuesday. You should let me in this time."

- Argument from Consequences

  - Arguing by showing the likelihood that good or bad (depending on your position) consequences will occur

  - Involves showing the links between what you are arguing and the consequences that you suggest

Yet another common reasoning practice for everyday argumentative situations, the argument from consequences, provides the specific good or bad consequences that could happen or are likely to happen for the particular action or decision. This could be equated to creating a pro and con chart when making a personal decision. The provision of the probable consequences connected to the evidence of those consequence or the evidence that supports the likelihood of those consequences can make a strong argument. An example of arguing from consequences may look like this:

A new bill introduced into the legislature calls for the reduction of speed limits throughout the state to 45 mph or less, depending on location.

Supporters of the bill argue that this is a good idea because the lower speed limits would lessen injuries in accidents, provide higher mpg output of the autos, and lessen the amount of auto accidents in the state. It is important to remember that appropriate evidence should be provided to support each consequence attributed to the claim.

- Argument from Expert Opinion

  - Showing that there are experts or professionals who agree with what you are arguing or support what you are arguing.

  - The experts have generally examined the evidence for and against and made their decision based on their status as experts

  - You must show that they are indeed experts

Argument from expert opinion essentially has an expert who is known to make true statements make a statement in support of the asserted claim. However, the argument from expert opinion can be a tricky one. Anyone who has watched a trial or a law based television show has seen multiple experts whose opinions contradict one another. With the mindset that no individual can be an overall expert in all things, it is more likely that the title of expert be given to people in a limited field of study or practice. As such, there can still be the issue of contradiction, but that is where the burden falls to the person asserting the claim to provide more evidence than the opposition. An argument from expert opinion may look like the following:

My car battery has died. I have the battery replaced. One day later, my car battery dies again. I go to an auto mechanic. A young man who is interning with the shop owner says that the problem is in the connections from my battery to my engine. The shop owner who has been a mechanic for 40 years and has multiple degrees in auto engine repair says that the problem is with the alternator, which is responsible for charging the battery when the motor is running and it should be replaced. When I ask my parents for the money to fix the car, I must convince them that the money for the alternator is necessary, even though the monetary outlay for replacing the cables is much smaller. I support my claim with the reasoning that the shop owner is an expert in his field and thus is far more likely to be correct in his diagnosis.

- Argument from Popular Practice

    - Showing that a large percentage of people or of the population is already doing or thinking what you are arguing.

    - You must show that most people or a large portion of people are doing or thinking what you are arguing

One must be careful when arguing from popular practice. It is easy to shift from popular practice to popular opinion, which can be a fallacy of logic and is not often considered valid. However, when crafted well, the argument from popular practice can be useful. In general I take more time working through the issues with this line of reasoning than with the others, as weakened arguments can easily arise out of this kind of reasoning. An argument from common practice may take the following form:

Students have been told that having headphones in their ears in the hallway during the school day is prohibited. It is only appropriate before and after school or at lunchtime. After a student has been assigned a consequence for having one headphone in and one headphone dangling from the set, that student argues that most students in the building use their headphones in the same way without incident. They further argue that with only one headphone in their ears between classes, students are aware of their surroundings, other students, and faculty that may need to speak to them. The student argues that they should not receive a consequence for the actions that match what most others are doing as well.

I generally include the idea of the slippery slope for many reasons. One of the main reasons is that the concept seems to come up often during reasoning discussions. Many students have heard the idea of a slippery slope from television or literature, and thus are interested in learning more about it.   I include it as a bridge between logical argumentative reasoning and fallacies of logic.

The Slippery Slope

- Argument showing causation from one point to another
- Shows a chain of multiple causes and events which lead from a starting point to a less obvious ending point
- Can easily teeter between reasoning and fallacy of reasoning

The argument form slippery slope requires multiple links of causation from the original act to an ending that is not clearly foreseeable from the outset. Often, the links in the chain of causation are not all complete or are not strong independently. Together, however the causes can make a compelling case. The struggle with the slippery slope is making sure that all of the causal links are clear and as strong as they can be. It is important to make sure that no liberties are taken with these links and that evidence is provided for each point in the causal flow. A common slippery slope argument may look like the following:

A parent has discovered their 13 year old child smoking cigarettes. In order to show the child the possible bad outcomes from inappropriately using items which are clearly illegal either in general or for their age group, the parent may provide a slippery slope type of argument.

1.   *Child illegally uses cigarettes*

2.   *Child sees no ill effects from doing something that is illegal.*

3.   *Child begins to drink alcohol because they did not see ill effects from other product (cigarettes) that are illegal for their age group but legal when older.*

4.   *Child tries marijuana as they have become desensitized to the protections that laws provide from certain substances.*

5.   *Child changes peer groups based on using these drugs that older people generally partake in.*

6.   *Child tries heroin due to pressure from the new peer group and desensitization to legality of substances.*

7.   *Child overdoses on heroin at the age of 15.*

This is a common argument that parents use with children and is a style of argument that is used in the battle for the legalization of marijuana. Although this is a possible outcome to these actions, the burden of proof and evidentiary support is large. It may be easy for someone arguing in opposition to negate one or more causal links and render the argument fallacious.

As with the evidence stage of learning about argument, the reasoning piece of argumentation education is the perfect place to speak to students about their metacognitive awareness. At these steps, students should incorporate an ongoing internal conversation in which they determine if their argument is taking shape in a way that can and will convince the intended audience. As with any type of writing, students must ask themselves questions regarding the purpose of their writing and if they are accomplishing their goals in a complete and effective manner.

The slippery slope is a good way to bridge between logical arguments and logical fallacies. After examining the common reasoning patterns I have chosen, examining the slippery slope and discussing the obvious issues that generally arise in discussion of the example, I then also speak to other reasoning fallacies that students should avoid. This helps to stop some common issues in reasoning that many people appeal to in everyday discussion and debate. This is also a good time to point out some differences between scientific argumentation and debate overall, especially the emotional appeal aspects of debating. These fallacies of logic often involve a lack of evidence. Oddly enough, that is the most prominent issue regarding students' arguments. This is a key discussion to have with students regarding evidence and reasoning. As students generally substitute their ideas of reasoning in places where data is actually needed, they then often lack much real evidence to support their ideas. This has been a pervasive issue with my students even after multiple discussions to resolve the issue. However, this preemptive discussion should not be omitted in the process of teaching reasoning patterns and argumentation.   It looks something like the following:

Fallacies of Reasoning – Avoid these

- Slippery Slope - arguing that a small or insignificant issue will eventually lead to a major result or consequence

The slippery slope is the perfect bridge between appropriate reasoning patterns and fallacious reasoning attempts. The slippery slope often attempts to show a string of causal events that lead to an ending event which is loosely related to the original supposed causal event. The ending event is often not connected at all or the arguer has taken great leaps or liberties in arriving at the final effect. The slippery slope is easily dispelled by approaching the weakest logical link, after which the entire train of links falls apart.

- Using Anecdotal Evidence – Substituting personal experience or stories for factual evidence

This is a common practice when arguing socio-scientific issues. Personal experience can be used as an introduction or in a conclusion to an argumentative essay, but as specific evidence, it is not acceptable on its own. In discussions regarding the appropriate evidence for each teacher's specific field, the appropriate sources of evidence should have been discussed. This is a good point in the argumentation education process to reiterate the evidentiary burden for the content area.

- Drawing Hasty Conclusions - makes an argument with only a small amount of evidence or data

Another distinct issue amongst students learning the argumentative process is the amount of evidence that is provided in support if their claim. Students far too often give one piece of evidence, then spend two or three sentences explaining it and go directly to their conclusion. Without the proper evidence, their reasoning has become fallacious in nature, even though there may be enough evidence to support it somewhere; it has just not been given in the argument.

- False Cause - argues that something has caused something else without evidence of that connection

The false-cause can have more than one source. A possibility is that a student has misinterpreted the data/evidence. This can arise in experimental science content areas as well as mathematical ones. This can come from a lack of knowledge or understanding of the content being used in the argument. This can also come from students making assumptions rather than trusting appropriate evidence. Also, I tend to apply this fallacy of reasoning to students' arguments that use inappropriate evidence for the field of study. Causation is important in scientific and socio-scientific arguments and the false-cause fallacy of reasoning must be avoided by students in their arguments.

- Suppressing Evidence - drawing a conclusion after purposely leaving out evidence or ignoring known evidence that might contradict a claim

Unfortunately, this is another fallacy of reasoning that we see in the realm of science. This is also one of the most common misleading notions that students will encounter in their adult life. Thereby, in the course of discussions and practice regarding reasoning misappropriations, this can have particular power with students. It is important to work with students to realize that suppressing evidence, although common in social and other real life situations, is dishonest and inappropriate in the classroom setting.

- Appeal to Unknown Authority - arguing a claim should be accepted based only on the suggestion that anonymous authorities accept the same idea or claim that they are making

This is another fallacy of reasoning that is common in social situations from the real world. It can also appear in social studies, science, and literature classes. This is a common fallacy of reasoning regarding interpretation. When one appeals to the unknown authority they may be remembering something someone said or maybe even real evidence that they have read or seen, however, evidence must be legitimate and substantiated. Too many times in common events people say things like, "You know what they say," or "People say." Old wives tales, or "common knowledge," are things that are often substitutes for real evidence. Appeals to unknown authorities are very often used to disguise a mere opinion of the author.

- Stereotyping – Arguing that something belonging to a group takes on all qualities associated with that group

Stereotyping appears in many form of reasoning. Stereotyping can appear in scientific reasoning, social studies, language arts, and in real life social argument situations. This is another time when a fruitful discussion can take place about the true nature of this ineffective and inappropriate form of reasoning. Also, the specific use of real and legitimate evidence provides no place for stereotyping.

- Ad Hominem – attacking the person making an argument rather than the facts or the argument

This is often an effort to counter an argument when no real evidence can be found to negate a person's stance. Once again, this is something that students will encounter in their lives outside of school and especially in their adult lives. The use of legitimate evidence cannot be overstated with regards to effective arguing and, more importantly, critical thinking. This is another discussion to have with students in which they realize that they must think about their own argument and their thinking regarding the effectiveness of their argument. Metacognitive discussions are important to have with students during both the evidence and reasoning phases of learning how to argue.

- Non Sequitur – attempting to link multiple ideas that have no logical connection

This is another reasoning fallacy that generally would not be an issue if the important metacognitive thinking is taking place. If the evidence that is necessary to show causation for a claim is not present, then that claim should not be made. That is one of the key conversations to have with the content before making an assertion or continuing with a poor claim. In the "constructing a Claim" scaffold, the student is asked if their claim can be supported with evidence. If there is no connection between ideas, causal or otherwise, then no assertion should be made, as even a semi-skilled arguer would counter that argument rather easily.

- Appeal to Fear – Trying to win by instilling fear of something rather than proving a point

Although emotional appeals can be useful, as long as they are an argument from consequences and supported succinctly by appropriate evidence, the appeal to fear is often another form of last resort effort when there is not sufficient evidence to support a claim, and the emotional reasoning of fear is used in place of that missing evidence. Emotional appeals are generally left to the field of debate and socio-scientific topical arguments. In scientific argumentation, whether it is in a science classroom or in one of the other content areas, the burden of proof must be met with field appropriate evidence that is legitimate and clearly supports the asserted claim.

- False Analogy – Assuming because things are similar in some ways that they must be similar in other ways or all ways

The fallacious reasoning of the false analogy is one that often comes from someone who does not have enough knowledge or understanding of what they are arguing. Looking at two things and seeing similarities is appropriate, but the arguer should have the critical assessing skills to see if those similarities are appropriate for supporting the similarities or assertions made in their claim. Once again, without sufficient and suitable evidence, a counterpoint may easily refute the original claim.

After presenting the reasoning patterns and fallacies of reasoning, it is a good time to go back through the entirety of what students have learned and apply their knowledge to new and different situations. The first three steps in scientific argumentation are pivotal

to the overall argument itself. These are what I call "The Big Three."
Although the counterargument and rebuttal are the more difficult
pieces of the concept and will help the most with students' critical
thinking skills, the argument itself is based and supported in the first
three phases.   Discussions with students regarding how to construct
claims, collect and sort evidence, and connect their evidence to their
claims are the main foci of multiple argumentative scaffolds. Modeling
and talking through the processes will help students to see the ways in
which evidence and reasoning should be critically assessed.

The importance of practicing argument specific activities in
conjunction with argumentative style thinking in multiple aspects of
the classroom cannot be overemphasized. As students practice as
often as possible, the specific foci of critical thinking and critically
assessing both evidence and the reasoning used in argument should
be taught through explicit instruction and specific practice, also. A
stimulating practice I engage in with students is rating the arguments
of others. I developed a rating scale that is essentially a rubric for
students to use as they examine arguments I have selected for them
to work with. I can choose arguments that are in different stages of
success and arguments that highlight specific issues based on the
progress of small groups or the entire class. I have, on many
occasions, written these arguments myself. In these instances, I can
help the students in situations where they are working with the
information that I wanted them to have, as well as approach their
argumentation skills. This is one of my trusted and go-to practice as it
serves multiple purposes and is far better than having students do
worksheets in which they rarely focus cognitively in order to complete.

So What? What are the reasons your Evidence and Data Prove your Claim?

Why is this evidence legitimate? Why should it be trusted? What about the source makes it appropriate to use as data/evidence?	Evidence/ Data	Why does this data/evidence support your claim? What is the logical connection between your data/evidence and your claim? What is the overall reasoning pattern
Why is this evidence legitimate? Why should it be trusted? What about the source makes it appropriate to use as data/evidence?	Evidence/ Data	Why does this data/evidence support your claim? What is the logical connection between your data/evidence and your claim? What is the overall reasoning pattern
Why is this evidence legitimate? Why should it be trusted? What about the source makes it appropriate to use as data/evidence?	Evidence/ Data	Why does this data/evidence support your claim? What is the logical connection between your data/evidence and your claim? What is the overall reasoning pattern

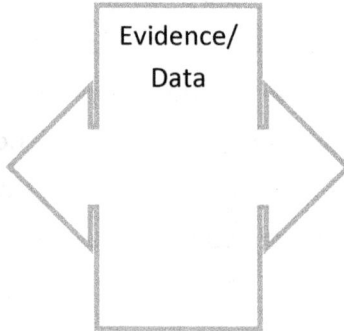

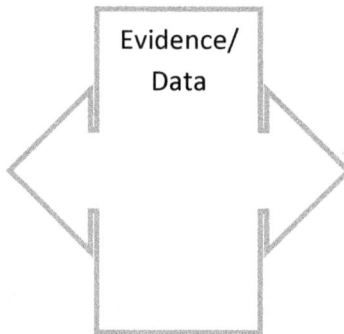

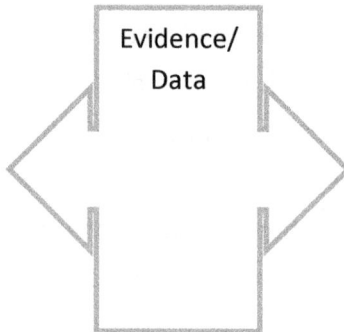

STEP 4: Critical Assessment and Metacognitive Thinking

In my experience in education, I have heard countless times that students need critical thinking skills. I have been told to teach critical thinking and have even read in teaching manuals that I needed to be teaching critical thinking. However, in all of that time, I have never had one individual tell me how exactly I am supposed to teach critical thinking skills to my students. I have been to countless training sessions and innumerable staff development meetings but the elusive knowledge of how to impart critical thinking skills in my students' minds was still lost to me. I even consulted educational journals and literature for the specifics of critical thinking and determined quickly that almost every source I consulted had significant trouble defining the concept. Within the peer reviewed literature and trade magazines from the fields of social studies, science, and reading education, there were multiple vague descriptions of what critical thinking is. It was not until the end of my doctoral coursework that a feminism studies doctoral candidate helped me to realize my own definition of critical thinking. My definition of critical thinking is the main reason that I refer to the concept most often as critical assessment. I also see critical thinking as being inextricably connected to metacognitive thinking. It is difficult to have one without the other.

I view critical thinking as the same process that a person goes through in creating an argument fully and also the process one goes through when they assess the argument of another. Critical thinking is being able to see all sides of a situation, examine the sources of evidence and their motivations, examine the source of power and who has the power, look for what is unheard, unseen, and unintended, look for those without a voice and hear what they would say, to find the relationships and responsibilities, and to get to the truth and the facts, whatever they may be. Perhaps most of all, critical thinking is being aware of the personal opinions and biases that you as an individual bring to your study or learning about anything. When a person thinks critically they are constantly questioning themselves, the situation, the data, and they are always carrying on conversations with their sources, their ideas, and their own mind. They are always thinking about their thinking as they are reasoning through critical assessments. You cannot have one without the other. And with argumentation, you can have it all. With argumentation, you must have it all.

Critical thinking contributes to most pieces of the argumentative process. Many of these points are addressed in the "constructing a claim" scaffold. As students construct a claim, one of the things that they must examine is whether or not there are other claims that may be similar to theirs. In order to do that, the arguer must look closely at multiple perspectives in the evidence. When constructing their claim, this will be superficial; the search for data and the reasoning that connects that data to the claim will allow students to more closely examine how the critical aspects of data and evidence connect to the plausibility of a claim. This shows clearly how the process of argumentation is an iterative progression that operates on a continuum until it is complete. As data, evidence, and reasoning are assessed and reassessed, it may at times be necessary to return to the claim or other pieces in order to solidify the ultimate argument which is complete and concrete. It is through the critical assessment and the metacognition which goes along with the process that an argument without holes through which the opposition can attack can be built.

The presence of evidence is also a part of constructing the claim. As one looks to decide on the specifics of the claim, students must be sure that there is appropriate evidence to support that claim. At the outset, the examination of the evidence may not be deep. Students can use data from observations, readings, history, or other basic sources in order to get started. As they continue through the process, they will often work back and forth along the continuum. This evaluation of evidence is an important place to examine the critical thinking involved in the process. One of the specific necessities with regard to evidence is its legitimacy. In order to examine the legitimacy of evidence, one must examine the source of that evidence and the legitimacy of that source. Not every piece of evidence is effective or appropriate for supporting a claim. There are some questions students can use to guide their thinking as they examine their evidence. These questions help students to have the internal metacognitive conversations that maintain and support critical assessment. These questions give the thinker specific ways to be skeptical of what they are reading, hearing, and seeing.

What is skepticism in a critical assessment?

When examining information and the source of that information, it is important to look on the things that you are learning with a healthy dose of skepticism. What that means is that you do not accept things as a fact or as truth without thinking about where the information is coming from and how it relates to what else you know about the subject.

As you examine your sources and evidence it is important that you closely and critically assess the validity, integrity, and status of the source. Critical assessment involves answering these questions regarding your information.

1.   Is the source of the evidence in a position to know about the subject matter?

2.   Is there a possibility of bias in the source of information?

3.   How does the information compart to other sources?

4.   Can the information be substantiated/corroborated?

5.   Does someone benefit from this information? If so, who?

6.   Does this information contradict other information?

7.   Is the source in a position of power or weakness?

8.   Is the source an original source or is this secondhand?

9.   What might an opposing source say?

10.   What point of view is absent or unheard?

When you examine a source, you should think about how the source itself is situated amongst the current understandings in the field.

- **Is the source accepted in the field as expert or legitimate information?**

    o **Is this peer reviewed literature?**

    o **Is this source filed literature?**

    o **Is this how people in the field get their information?**

- **How does the information from the source compare to other information in the field?**

    o **Can the information be corroborated by other field sources?**

    o **Does the information match other information in the field?**

    o **Is this information in opposition to other information in the field?**

- **Is this a primary or secondary source?**

  - o **If the source is primary, you must examine the motivations of the author.**

  - o **If the source is secondary, you must examine the motivation and process of the person(s) responsible for the interpretation of the original evidence**

- **Was the source written from a position of power or weakness?**

  - o **Sources written from a position of power often are one sided and present the views only of those in power.**

  - o **Sources written from a position of weakness can be biased in order to convince.**

  - o **Sources from a position of weakness may be difficult to interpret.**

  - o **When only sources from a position of power are found, it is important to look for the voice of those that are not heard.**

What might others that have been silenced by those in power think or have to say

- **Is there a plausible alternative that has not been described or written about?**

When examining and critically assessing the source of information, the motivations of the sources are extremely important things to consider when determining what sources are legitimate.

When examining the evidence and its source, these questions allow students to critically assess evidence so there are no holes in this important part of the argument. With these questions, they can help themselves to be cognizant regarding the legitimacy of their sources. Once they have determined that their evidence is authentic and reasonable, they can move on to connecting that evidence to the claim through their reasoning with confidence. The critical thinking questions and the methodologies students should use to properly answer these questions should be taught explicitly, practiced, and explored through discussion and modeling. These are the pivotal questions which help students to develop these critical thinking skills. At this stage of learning about argument, students should have practiced these skills already and thus you can point out how they have already been successful in their development process. These questions and skills can be applied across any curriculum area and most importantly in their lives holistically. This way of thinking and

approaching new information will suit students well as they enter the
real world. If they can approach new things with these points in mind,
they can learn whatever they need to learn and do it well. In their
journey, though, they will also need to monitor their adherence to
these questions and the way in which they approach the process. The
reason this procedure is most effective when implemented here is the
fact that it is necessary to follow this process in order to get the win.
The progression should happen each and every time and when this
kind of thinking is interwoven into the classroom environment, it will
become second nature to students.

The metacognitive thinking that students focus on to develop
successful habits with critical thinking can be taught through modeling
and think alouds. The act of students monitoring their own thinking
and thought processes is of utmost importance. It is through the
metacognitive process that students develop for themselves (with the
help of a knowledgeable teacher) that they become independent
critical thinkers and learners. Students are far more adept at
pinpointing their own weaknesses. If they choose, they are in tune to
their own flaws and fortes. They can be trusted to identify what they
are lacking and where their issues generally arise. We must empower
them to do so. By giving them questions to ask themselves as they go
through their thinking, we help to begin this metacognitive
development. Through our own modeling and scaffolding, we help
students identify what works for them and what does not. Individual
conferences with students can be very helpful as they work this out. I
often conference with students while others are engaged in research,
small group discussion, and the process of reading, writing, and rating
arguments.

Metacognitive Questions about the individual Arguer's Approach

1. What are my assumptions going into this learning?

2. What are my biases?

3. What background knowledge do I have? Do I need more in order to understand my sources?

4. What are my questions for the source or its author?

5. Do I understand what I am reading? Can I summarize it in my own words?

6. What do I need to do in order to be as clear as possible about what I am researching?

7. How do I know I am accurate in my answers to the previous questions?

8. Have I followed the appropriate methodology for critical assessment of my sources?

9.   Am I on track for developing a legitimate argument?

These basic metacognitive comprehension and thinking
questions can help students train themselves to determine their level
of understanding and help them see when the need for further
investigation, outside resources, or help from another person.
Although the explicit instruction in critical thinking and metacognitive
thinking can be interwoven throughout the instructional and practice
sessions, after the Big 3 have been presented is a good time to focus
on how these processes all fit together. It is also a possibility, should
you choose, to introduce this explicit instruction in the beginning of
argumentative instruction or anywhere else you see fit. After all, you
are a professional and you know your students.

Step 5: See the Counterargument

The Counterargument

What it is:

This is where you think of positions or claims that others may have against your argument.

This is where you determine what someone who doesn't agree with you might believe.

This is where you determine why others might have a different opinion

Questions to Ask Yourself:

What is an alternate point of view to my claim?

Why might someone believe is an alternate point of view for the subject matter?

What evidence might someone give to support an alternate claim?

The fact is, as you are practicing what I refer to as the "Big 3," creating a claim, getting your evidence together, and connecting your claim to your evidence through reasoning, it is pivotal to point out the successes student are having with their development of argumentative prowess, critical assessment, and metacognition. Teachers and students will struggle with this new approach to learning and thinking. However, as I previously stated, the struggle is where the progress is made. So as they grapple, students may need more encouragement than in other scenarios. The payoff is well worth it. They need to see and hear when they are being successful, and they will be successful. You will be proud. They will be proud.

One reason that it is crucial for students to understand your definition and expectations as far as critical thinking and metacognition are concerned is that as you venture into the counterargument piece of the puzzle critical thinking is the main ingredient.

To present the most effective argument, the arguer must suitably see alternate opinions, explanations, points of view, and arguments. In a similar but different way than students approach the critical assessment of evidence and the sources of evidence students here must see their argument and the subject matter from multiple points of view. There are many sides to every story, and to accurately predict a counterargument you must try and see as many as possible. As I tell my students, the counterargument is not *the* opposing or opposite view or idea, it is *another* viewpoint or idea. A perfect example of this happens when I venture through the oceanic biozone with Oceanography students. When we discuss the adverse effects that humans have on the coastal and oceanic environments, it is difficult for the students to see an opposite point of view. It is illogical to state that the depletion of fish species through overfishing or the manual erosion of the coastal environment through tourists collecting materials from beaches is a good thing. The damage is clear and, although it is likely there is someone in the world that states that this is good, once again, in general this is illogical. The first inclination students have is to merely state the opposite viewpoint and then supply the same evidence that they have in their original argument to rebut that counterargument. I take them through the idea that counter is not always opposite. In this case, the counterargument could be that the economic benefits currently outweigh the possible long term environmental issues. This is generally a very eye opening discussion for them.

Essentially that little story sets us up for the actuality of introducing the counterargument. Through a majority of studies and from my own experience with students it is clear that this is the most often overlooked piece of creating a solid argument. This always intrigues me because I know for a fact that it is generally taught in language arts when they touch on the argumentative essay. It is a pivotal part of debate. Even when I absolutely require this of students by making it a part of the rubric, having the concept thoroughly explained in graphic organizers for their argument, and going over possible ways to determine the counterargument, I will have 15%-20% of my students present me with an argument that contains no allusion at all to a possible alternative point of view. It is these students that I conference with individually and work with to point out the need for a counterargument in their work. With a somewhat small number of students exhibiting this issue, I can do this while the other students peer evaluate their arguments.

When introducing the concept of the counterargument, one should attempt to prevent the mindset that this is like constructing another entire argument on a small scale. However, as students may begin to see it that way, they can be gently nudged towards the realization that their actual ground work for the counterargument is done as they critically assess the evidence for their argument. The idea of counterargument is, once again, *an* opposing viewpoint. Therefore, as students research their evidence in support of their claim, they will likely come across alternate ideas and viewpoints. As you introduce the idea of the counterargument, which I do at the beginning of a unit or argumentative assignment so they can actually look for this evidence during the process, it is important to demonstrate how you identify the alternate viewpoints. With the sufficient training and practice that has certainly taken place in your classroom regarding the critical assessment of information and evidence, it should nearly be second nature for students to see the alternate viewpoints and the evidence that may support them.

Students can make note of this in the counterargument and rebuttal scaffold during the research process, thereby saving themselves exponential amounts of time as they progress through counterargument and rebuttal. What is also very important as students advance is for them to determine what works for them and what they will be able to make habitual. So as they are reading and research, I have them think of the ideas which a counterargument represents:

Constructing the Counterargument

This is where you think of positions or claims that others may have different from your argument.

- *This is where you determine what someone who doesn't agree with you might believe.*

- *This is where you determine why others might have a different opinion*

- *This is where you locate the evidence that someone who holds an alternate opinion would use as backing for that claim*

As you did your original research, it is likely that you came across some information as well as some ideas that were different or in opposition to the claim that you have made. The counterarguments that you

***should include in your total argumentative approach
come from these alternate views.***

***As you construct your argument, you should
consider these alternative points of view, consider
the evidence and reasoning which support them, and
make attempts to fully understand how these points
of view could be presented as alternate claims.***

Practice in locating counterarguments during the research process
will train students to see opposing views. This is another piece of
critical thinking. Seeing alternate ideas and alternate viewpoints
allows students to stay open minded and be more prepared to learn
new things in school and in the world outside of the classroom.   It is
this kind of critical thinking that is important across all content areas.
Students should spend some time in pairs and in small groups helping
each other to broaden their points of view. These groups should be as
diverse as possible. When discussing with students, one can also point
out that the more a person knows, the better able they are to adjust
their viewpoints and see from multiple positions. Each and every
learning experience alters our vantage point towards the world in
which we live. Therefore, even the most menial task is one that we
can take lessons and more experience from. All activities are
important in some way for someone. I often take time at this point to
also discuss the attention to detail in all tasks that successful students
have. It is important for them to approach activities with focus and
curiosity in order to get the best from themselves and others. These

are the skills that they will use in life every day. I take the time to point that out with vigor.

In the language arts classroom, the ideas of counterargument and multiple points of view are an essential skill for interpreting and writing literature. It has often been said that the best literature, the literature that is timeless, appeals to so many people because it fits so many possible interpretations that each person can read and make it their own. The writing of good literature calls for seeing what is written through the possible perspective from which that literature will be interpreted. Writing quality literature goes hand in hand with interpreting many kinds of literature. With that in mind, as students work to develop appropriate interpretations of literature and provide the evidence required to support their interpretations, the act of working to see other possible interpretations and the evidence that supports them, contributes to students' abilities for both reading and writing. For teachers, scientific argumentation with regards to literature can be an invaluable tool to help students develop the interpretation skills as well as the writing skills that will benefit them in their futures.

Similarly, in the social studies classroom, the interpretations of historical events and the primary sources that detail those events can take on an experience that is similar to these same acts with regards to literature. The process of critically assessing of primary source documents as literature and as history necessitates an approach which sees multiple viewpoints. Students must approach the stories, explanations, and past interpretations of history with skepticism and as much experience as they can. Each time they learn something new, they are adding to the understandings with which they approach interpreting new experiences. The specific questions from the critical thinking and metacognitive section can help students to dig deep enough to see the alternate viewpoints and the evidence that may support them. They can then determine which viewpoint is more likely to be appropriate and how to convince others of their interpretation. It is, however, the process of assessing the multiple possibilities and stories that *could* be true with skepticism that makes those in the social sciences great thinkers. Reading and learning is always adding to their repertoire and molding their mindset to include more and more possibilities. In social sciences every experience is an addition to the overall critical thinking ability of anyone who chooses to learn with focus and purpose. Overall, the new focus on counterargument continues the development of critical thinking skills. Doing the same kinds of metacognitive and critical assessment during research for data and in the counterargument phase essentially gives a kind for double training and practice in quality thinking.

Scientists are always looking for theories which better explain what evidence or observations they have come across. Science is about understanding and explaining the world around us and as such, there are often conflicting attempts at explanation. Although when one does research to help shore up their scientific understandings of the pieces to a theory or experiment from which a fully complete claim or assertion should result, a focus on what the counterclaim could and should be may have students dig just a little bit farther. In my experience with my 8th grade physical science students, I recall more than a few students referring to the fact that they did dig deeper because they wanted to make sure that they understood the other point of view (or points of view) enough to rebut them well. Their focus on winning and being right lead them through a deeper understanding of the topic in general and better critical thinking regarding what was possible and what multiple assessments might determine.   As with the connection between the language arts style of thinking and the social studies approach, there is a link with the thinking that takes place in the sciences as well. When teaching these ideas, it can be helpful and effective if there are more teachers involved across the curriculum areas so that students see the thinking works well in all aspects of their studies. If that is not possible, it may benefit all parties involved if you work to help students realize how well the thinking that they are developing with you thorough argumentation can be used in all subject areas and in most aspects of their adult life. I don't believe that the real life application of scientific argumentation can be oversold. Students question most assignments as to their benefits in the real world. This is a way of thinking and approaching understanding that will indeed be used throughout a person's life and in interactions with people in the world around us.

The counterargument itself is a way to experience alternate points of view. In developing a counterargument, thinkers are essentially forced to dig deeper into the process and take a step back from the information, from their own opinions (whether they are developed or previously held), and from any bias they may have, or have developed, in order to see alternate viewpoints. Critically assessing data and evidence goes even deeper when the critical thinking of counterargument is added to the necessary research and metacognitive exercises. It is clear that working along the continuum of the argument is demonstrated thoroughly from claim to counterargument. Thinkers can examine their choices and research as new ideas and evidence come to light through these thinking exercises, sometimes this will involve going back to the research or looking for more research.

An Alternate Assessment of the situation: The Counterargument

The counterargument is an alternate claim, data/evidence, and reasoning pattern which attempts to explain the same thing that you are attempting to explain. In to fully solidify an argument, you must also examine alternate proposals or possibilities.

What is an alternate point of view to my claim? What claim can be made from this point of view that offers an alternate explanation/theory to mine?	
What date/evidence is there which supports this alternate claim?	Why might someone believe the alternate point of view for the subject matter? What reasoning might connect the data/evidence to the alternate claim?

Step 6: The Rebuttal

The Rebuttal

What it is:

This is how you convince others who hold opposing view that your view is correct.

This is how you show that opposing points of view are invalid or incorrect.

This is where you show why opposing evidence is invalid or does not support opposing claims

Questions to Ask Yourself:

Why are alternate views not correct?

What evidence shows that my claim is more valid or more correct than the alternate claims?

Why is the evidence supporting alternate views incorrect?

Why is the science supporting alternate views not appropriate to support those claims?

If the other portions of scientific argumentation have been thoroughly completed, the rebuttal is not complicated or difficult. It can be considered the home stretch and the ease of completing it may feel like a reward for students working in your classrooms. After the critical assessment of the information and the critical thinking that goes into the development of the counterargument, students should be at the highest level of understanding from their research, reading, and writing. With their thorough command of the evidence in support of their claim, the ideas represented in the counterclaim and their effective reasoning about the entire picture, they simply have to now determine what evidence or reasoning is best to defeat the counterclaim.

The position of the counterclaim is an alternate theory, an alternate idea, an alternate interpretation, or just an alternate view to what your claim is. Thus there must be a reason that someone may think that position is the most accurate, correct, or definitive. Once the support for the counterargument has been established, likely through the research previously done and the critical thinking done in the actual determination of the counterargument, the arguer must discern ways to negate either that evidence or the reasoning. In some cases, the evidence itself may not be enough to satisfy the burden of proof, in which case the arguer need merely to point that out. In other cases, the data may not be plentiful enough. No matter what the circumstances, it is the critical assessment that finds holes in data. When the arguer is creating their argument, they are spending the time and the cognitive energy to make sure that the data has been vetted for accuracy and validity. Sources of data have been checked in order to make sure they are indeed proper and experts have been examined to make sure they are knowledgeable enough to be considered experts in the field to which they are contributing. In examining their own data and sources of evidence, students have practiced the process that they will follow in order to contradict the support for alternate points of view. To find the cracks in the wall of data, arguers are looking for sources that should not be used, data that cannot be verified, lack of data/evidence, and all other data/evidence problems we have trained them to avoid in their own arguments supporting their claims.   Negating the data itself, can take on different forms depending on the content area.

In social studies, we look for bias, self-serving motivations, power struggles, lack of power, too much power, personal, political, and professional agendas, and other mitigating factors that may influence the source of data or the data itself. When examining first hand evidence or accounts of historical events, the critical viewpoints should be examined thoroughly. This gives another chance for students to review where support is coming from and where the alternate points or points of view are coming from. Modifications that could have been made to evidence and dependability of sources are other key places to look for weaknesses in counterarguments that can be exposed in rebuttal. When facing an opposing arguer, their bias can also be used against them.

Constructing the Rebuttal

While doing your research, building your evidence and reasoning, and examining the counterargument, you likely realized that there were problems with the points of view that were different than your claim. The rebuttal is the appropriate place in the construction of your argument to highlight these issues that likely kept you from supporting these alternate clams.

So as you have reasons that led you to your claim, also there were reasons that kept you from the others. Asking yourself certain questions can help you to pinpoint the issues with evidence or with reasoning patterns that can be used to rebut the counterclaims you have already identified.

Consider the Following in your search for the Rebuttal:

- *Is there enough evidence to show causation?*

- *Can the evidence be logically connected to the claim with an appropriate reasoning pattern?*

- *Is the evidence legitimate?*

- *Is there bias in the source?*

- *Does the evidence meet the same high standards that you expect of your own evidence?*

- *Is there any evidence missing?*

- *Is the logic and reasoning that would be used in support of the alternate claim fallacious?*

- *Has the theory and understanding been applied appropriately for the subject area?*

- *Does the reasoning actually apply to the situation?*

- *Is there a chance that you came to your conclusion in error and there is not a clear rebuttal for the alternate argument?*

In the sciences, data can create multiple issues for the arguer. This is good for identifying problems in the counterargument. As previously discussed, science has very specific rules for data and evidence. Experts in science fields must have credentials in order to be trusted for evidence. In addition, science journals used for evidence are generally peer reviewed. The peer policing process in sciences is strict and precisely regulated. Deviations from these rules in evidence supporting a counterargument should be pointed out as weaknesses in that counterargument.

In the field of language arts, evidence is generally the specific words of the author, understandings of the time period that the author has written, or specific biographical or interpreted information about the author. Bias within the possible interpretations of words and phrases and merely a lack of knowledge of the genre, content, or subject matter can also be holes to point out in data. Also, in literature, the basic underpinnings of literary interpretation can be faults in a counterargument. Improper understandings of grammar and figurative language are often specific errors made in devising evidence to support a claim. Overall, the basics of literary device are used as evidence and can thusly be places to search for problems in evidence.

The reasoning that connects the counterargument to the claim may also be an area of weakness used to defeat the assertion that it is meant to support. Overall, this is a great time to review the fallacies of logic students were warned to avoid. The rebuttal is a time to prove to them why it is so important to avoid these as they reason through their own argument, as you work with them to use these logical fallacies to rebut a counterargument. A quick review of the fallacies may not be a poor choice of ways to spend time. Determining examples to share with students with content related topics that they have already studied could be a great way to review past information and give them logic puzzles to figure out. Having them determine the fallacy of reasoning involved in a situation is a great logic puzzle to get them to think critically about situations involving that prior learning.

In science, faulty reasoning may include an inaccurate or inappropriate application of scientific law or theory. A trail of causation can also be faulty even if the data itself is accurate. Data can be misinterpreted from simple observation or also unsuitably connected to the claim. A common reasoning issue that comes up in science is using anecdotal evidence. In cases when a single experiment has been done or there is personal experience involved, an attempt can be made to substitute that for real scientific data. Also, without enough evidence to truly prove a theory or causation, the issue of drawing hasty conclusions happens often in science content arguments. Not having enough evidence yet still trying to prove the claim is simple to rebut because in that case, the one who is willing to do the groundwork and the research is going to have the better evidentiary proof. Another common issue is using evidence that is not rooted in true expert testimony or in actual science. Attempting to apply hearsay or anonymous data can be interpreted as the reasoning fallacy of appeal to unknown authority. This is common when, once again, the research is not done thoroughly and proper identification of the source of evidence has not been done. The evidence itself could be practical and appropriate, but there has been a breakdown in research or record-keeping, thus leading to a weakened counterargument.

In social studies, some similar fallacies can take place, however, sometimes the more personal or obtuse thinking fallacies apply. For example, stereotyping can be a significant fallacy when a counterargument or opposing position attempts to generalize thoughts or actions from one or a few individuals to an entire group. Also, stating that just because a person is a member of a group that they share all qualities of others in that group. In the social sciences, this can be a common fallacy of reasoning. I consider it a lazy way to argue or an easy road to a point that may not be a logical evidentiary connection. An appeal to fear can also be a veiled attempt to masque lack of evidence or causal connection in social studies. When participating in competitive argumentative sessions, this can be a fallacy involved in an alternative position, but it is also a fallacy sometimes used by arguers to try and rebut a counterargument. This fallacy is often born out of previous experience in debate or other social styles of argument. In scientific argumentation, hard evidence and logical reasoning are the rule and should be adhered to specifically.

Language arts is another social science and can thus also have similar issues regarding fallacies of logic. One of the most likely here, though, is the ad hominem fallacy. With such personal connections to authors in the interpretation of their work, focusing reasoning on the person instead of the argument or evidence can be something that happens adversely and sometimes without the realization of that fallacy by the arguer. With dependence on literary movements and time periods in support of evidence and as sources of evidence and reasoning, stereotyping and false analogies can be fallacies to look for (and avoid) in the interpretation of literature. As arguers and counterarguers are attempting to develop connections for their interpretations, grouping authors into movements or time periods may be a way to connect their points. However, it may take (again) better research to rebut these assertions. Also, showing the similarities in one way with the connections leads to similarities in other ways can be difficult to rebut. The answers are in the thinking and the research. It is the arguer with the most comprehensive understanding that will generally be successful.

The counterargument and the rebuttal bring together some of the best support for the importance of the research and critical assessment process. The initial research is significant in developing the claim and preliminary evidentiary basis, but it is the overall approach to reading, interpreting, comprehending, and focusing on the true assimilation of the information and context that absolutely force a deep and thorough experience with learning. The work, time, and attention to detail during research makes the rest of the argumentative process smoother. Once an iterative understanding is incorporated into a learner's consciousness, the process flows well. A true understanding of a topic means seeing it from multiple perspectives and being aware of trusted sources, expertise in that field, and context. The arguer's reasoning and understanding of counterarguments lead to the ease of rebuttal. Once the student has taken a stance and has the desire to prove that stance, the process becomes more personal and thus their intrinsic motivations are higher.

The Rebuttal: What is wrong with the Counterargument?

List the counterargument to your claim

What can you find wrong with the data/evidence, the legitimacy of that evidence, or the reasoning used to connect the data/evidence to the counterclaim?

Data/Evidence	
Why is it not legitimate?	Why is it not accurate or applicable?
What is the reasoning connecting this evidence to the claim?	
Why is the reasoning not warranted?	

Data/Evidence	
Why is it not legitimate?	Why is it not accurate or applicable?
What is the reasoning connecting this evidence to the claim?	
Why is the reasoning not warranted?	

Outline of Implementation

I.   Introduce the Claim as your idea and your assertion
    a.   What is Your assertion?
    b.   Be Explicit and Clear
    c.   Can you support it with Evidence?

II. Find the Data/Evidence to Support the Claim
    a.   Find evidence that is connected to the claim
    b.   Use multiple sources
    c.   Ask Why?Why?Why?
    d.   Critically Assess the Validity of the Evidence
    e.   Is it Valid, Legitimate, and supportive of the claim?

III. Develop Inductive and Deductive Reasoning Patterns
    a.   Reasoning Connects the Evidence to the Claim
    b.   IS the connection legitimate and supported by the evidence?
    c.   Argument Patterns
        i.   Analogy
        ii.   Established Rule
        iii. Precedent
        iv.   Consequences
        v.   Expert Opinion
        vi.   Popular Practice
        vii. The Slippery Slope
    d.   Fallacies of Reasoning
        i.   The Slippery Slope
        ii.   Anecdotal Evidentiary
        iii. Hasty Conclusions

        iv. False Cause

        v. Suppressing Evidence

        vi. Unknown Authority

        vii. Stereotyping

        viii. Ad hominem

        ix. Non Sequitur

        x. Appeal to Fear

        xi. False analogy

IV.   Critical Thinking and Metacognitive Thinking

    a. Question the Validity of Sources

    b. Question the Motivation of Sources

    c. Who has the power?

    d. Whose Voice is not heard?

    e. What is my stance?

    f. What is my bias?

    g. What is my level of understanding?

    h. Do I need help?

    i. Can I summarize?

V.   Counterargument

    a. An Alternate idea, stance, or theory

    b. Find through critical thinking and seeing multiple viewpoints

    c. What would someone who does not agree with me say?

VI.   Rebuttal

    a. Determine the Evidence and Reasoning in Support of the Counterclaim

    b. Devise a way to show evidence is not appropriate or sufficient

    c. Find fallacies or holes in the line of reasoning

VII.   PRACTICE, PRACTICE, PRACTICE

Chapter 6: Reading for Comprehension

"The more that you read, the more things you will know. The more that you learn, the more places you'll go."

— Dr. Seuss, I Can Read With My Eyes Shut!

"Reading furnishes the mind only with materials of knowledge; it is thinking that makes what we read ours."

— John Locke

Perhaps the greatest thing about having students venture into argumentation is the fact that is gives them purpose in whatever they are doing in the classroom. This purpose can often roll over into what they are doing outside of the classroom, which has always been my goal. When it comes to reading, however, it is the rationale with which students approach their reading that helps them to make the most sense from the words and ideas on the page. It has always been my understanding and experience that, if a person can read for understanding effectively, then they can learn just about anything they need or want to. If you can read for information and knowledge, there is nothing that can stand in your way with regard to accomplishing your goals. Reading is at the heart of all that we do. Argumentative thinking and learning gives students a goal for their reading and the need for understanding. It is not something that we as teachers are necessarily asking of them, it is something that they are asking of themselves in order to be successful. We do, however, have a responsibility to help our students read as effectively as possible. For us to do this, we must meet them at their level and bring them up to where they need to be. Some students will come to us with the skills and experience necessary to jump right in to the research and reading that they need to do. Others will not. It is for the teachers of those students that I include this section.

In any educational store, educational section of a bookseller, or even the educational section of a library, you could likely throw a handful of rocks and have most of them touch a book about reading or teaching reading. There are thousands of people who have made a comfortable living teaching others how to teach reading. I am not attempting to be exhaustive in my survey of reading strategies; I will merely offer what I have learned from my experience in higher education, my experience as a language arts teacher, and my experience in all of the other core content areas. As I implemented argumentative practices in my classroom, though, it was instantly clear that reading strategies would be necessary. For clarity I have attempted to group them effectively.

Our students need a wide variety of strategies from which they can pull effective practices for the different situations that they might encounter as they read. Practicing multiple approaches helps students to develop the vast array of tools that they may need. However, all of these schemes cannot be taught at once. It will take time to implement them in a way that students can use them effectively so that in time they can call these strategies their own. With this in mind, it may be practical to institute them when they seem most helpful, being careful to institute as many as possible multiple times throughout the course of your teaching. I have come to a point where I follow a rotation of these practices and substitute particular tactics situationally when they seem to fit better than others. I also explain my thinking and reasoning as to my choices of strategies. This may include the fact that I did not have a particular reason and I just chose a random strategy or my favorite. For example, the illustrated dictionary is my favorite general vocabulary strategy. I tell my students that and encourage them to let me know when I have overused it. I also allow them to make suggestions as to a strategy so that nothing becomes stale. I believe that the dialogue with my students is one of the things that makes my instruction effective. They need to understand my thinking and reasoning as to strategies, the use of those strategies, and generally all aspects of my teaching and personal learning. I know I am good at it and I want them to be also, so I let them see my processes as often as possible.

Vocabulary

I do not believe enough can be said about having an extensive vocabulary. One of the first things I try to instill in my high school students is that, aside from your appearance, your vocabulary and how you use it is one of the first things people notice about you. The use of certain words shape the way people treat you and moves you towards certain paths. It may not be fair for others to judge us on the things we say and how we say them, but it is a reality. I still quote the movie Dangerous Minds to my students several times a year. "Words are thoughts and we can't think without 'em." Vocabulary strategies are extremely important to developing reading abilities and successes in our students.

The first of these strategies isn't really a strategy. It is to have appropriate level dictionaries available for students. Collegiate dictionaries are all that I use. Many have come from yard sales and Goodwill stores. When I approach the subject of looking up words and the need for using dictionaries, I like to tell my students about my experiences in higher education. During the first two years of my Ph.D. studies, I kept a word document with all of the words that I had to continually look up. These words were so very new to me that I found myself looking them up multiple times because I did not remember the meaning or the context in which they were used. I encourage students to do the same thing as they are working with more research style words and higher level thinking words which they will inevitably interact with during their topical research. I have only had to require this once with my students. They were a special mixture of lazy and overly sensitive to their perceived intelligence levels. Once I show the students my personal dictionary from college, they seem to be more receptive to the idea.

In a controlled environment, previewing the more difficult content words makes a significant difference for all students, but especially for the ELL and SLD students. There are a multitude of pre-reading strategies which focus on vocabulary. The ultimate choice for each individual teacher, class, and possibly student should be what works. The groundwork by the teacher is to find the words that will likely give students issues or the words which truly embody the content. Once those words have been chosen, it is time to choose a strategy. The main point that I make with students before beginning any vocabulary strategy is that the definitions or understandings of the words should come through context.   If the textbook is the tool we are using then I outlaw the glossary. Students need to get their meaning and understandings from the context that the words are used in alongside their definitions. Sometimes we use field journals, magazine articles, or others content specific sources, but in any situation, it is the context that makes the word and that makes the meaning.

The first of my go-to strategies is the illustrated dictionary. The illustrated dictionary is exactly what it sounds like. Students define words and illustrate them. I always tell my students that defining the word and then creating some sort of illustration which depicts the meaning of the word allows them to use both hemispheres of their brains and thereby internalize the words more effectively. Although the illustrated dictionary can be modified to include more factors, I believe that the strength of this strategy is in its simplicity. Students can complete the dictionary on their own, in pairs or small groups, or the teacher can lead the way through especially difficult terminology.

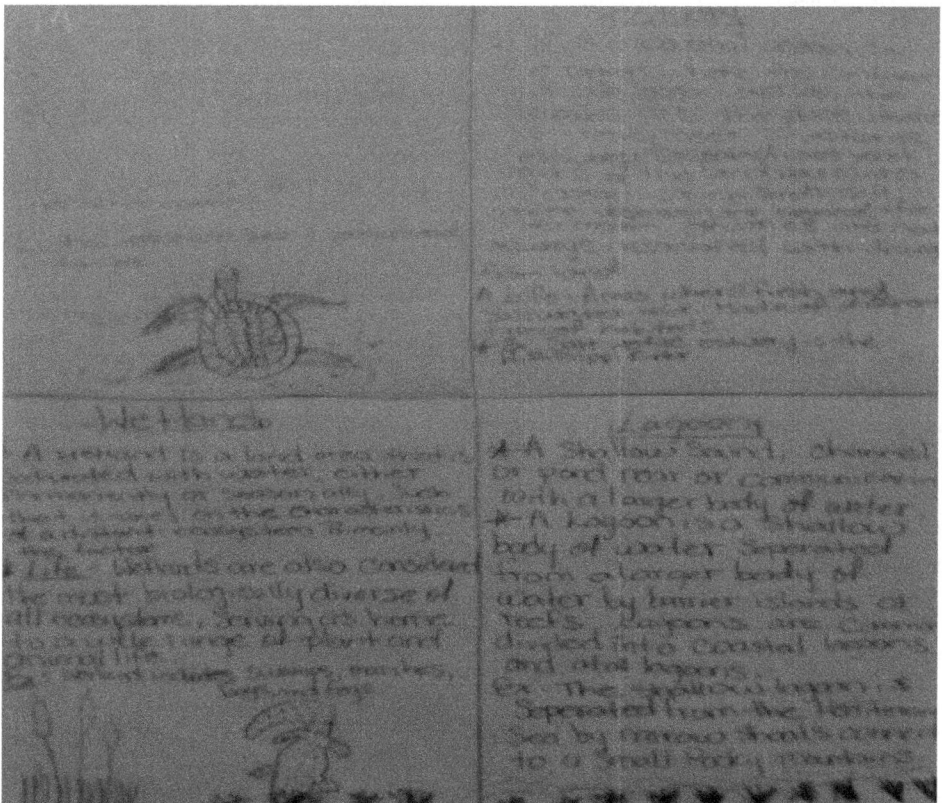

Another strategy that I use with words that are conceptual in nature is the word association technique. I sometimes call this four-square, but the general idea is the association of words and meaning. In this template the word is placed in the center of the four squares. In square 1, students write a definition. In square two they must use the word in a sentence that accurately depicts its meaning through usage. In the third square the students use words that are synonymous or associated with the chosen word. In the fourth square students write words which could be confused for words that are associated with the word or antonyms of the word. Essentially, they are writing what the word is not. This is especially helpful with words or concepts that are similar or use confusingly similar roots. It also helps students to see the concept or word in opposition to things that could be confusing about the word or concept.

Definition	Use in a sentence
What the word consists (or synonyms)	What the word isn't

Another vocabulary strategy that can be very useful while
students are engrossed in a unit is a connections chart.   With some of
the more complex topics in all of the content areas, there are those
ideals that have a plethora of new or important vocabulary. Even with
strategies that help students to understand the words, it is always
important for students to see how they relate to each other and the
overall concept. I most often have students draw these connections in
the same way as we might do a thinking map or a concept chart. In a
similar way as the Four-Square technique, this allows students to see
the connections between words and the way that the concepts feed
into, and off of, one another. The connections between individual
pieces of a concept and how they fit together can be a significant
challenge for students and using this strategy as they are researching
or working on reading for understanding in a vocabulary heavy
environment or subject area can be very helpful. Knowing the words
and how they fit together like puzzle pieces or how they influence

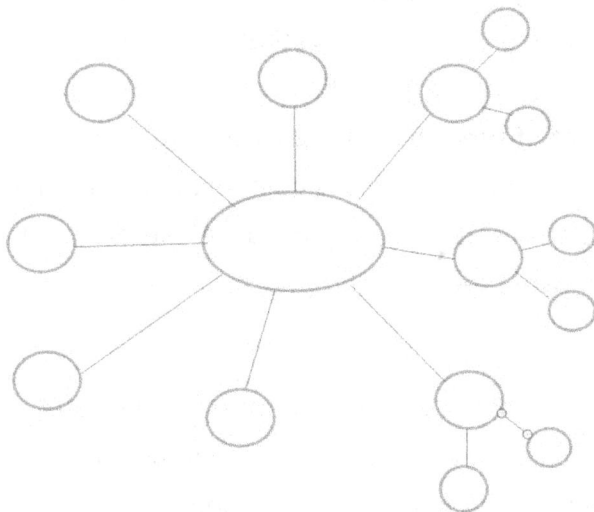

multiple facets of subject matter is beneficial to comprehension and retention.

The template can essentially look like whatever is necessary. The tool gives the teacher the ability to pre-design the concept connections for students so that they have a bit of a roadmap to fill in. Students can also create their own and then have discussions, or mini-arguments, to determine the most effective groupings. The thinking and the discussion are important to developing understandings. This can also make use of the differing amounts of background knowledge students possess.

Pre-Reading

Strategies that have students preview material in different ways are important for helping struggling readers and can also benefit any learner by speeding up the process of comprehension. For many readers a "cold reading" in which they open up a text or a website and start reading wastes a significant amount of time as they try to get the gist of what they are reading, place it into context, and then develop an understanding of the content that they can work with. Regardless of skill level, pre-reading strategies either save time or take about the same amount of time that the process would take without these strategies. The struggle is less complex and time used is better spent when these strategies are employed. All students benefit from these approaches, whether their comprehension is served or their interest is piqued.

A picture walk is likely the most used strategy in my arsenal. Although it is called a picture walk, it can be called a chapter walk, a section walk, or any kind of walk, depending on the text used. Essentially, readers get to "walk" through the text by flipping through the pages. During this time, readers look at pictures, read captions, examine bold and italicized words, ponder section headings and sub-headings, and scan the first sentence or two of each section to get a general idea of what the text will be about. This activity allows students to activate whatever background knowledge and schema that they have connected to the overall topic, gets them thinking about how the topic might connect to them personally or what they are trying to understand, helps them to identify words that might give them trouble as they read, and gives an overall scaffold for what they are reading. The students know what to expect and thus can adjust their mindset, thinking, and approach accordingly. For example, if a reader was "walking" through this chapter, they could easily see that the text is expository in nature and the goal revolves around reading strategies for students. The main headings such as *vocabulary*, *pre-reading, while your reading, and bringing it home* would identify the times when the strategies are employed and could easily draw a reader's attention to a specific set of strategies that they may need. I can only assume that is how the reader has approached this book from the outset of their experience. I know that is how I read. As a "walker" might examine further, they could easily skim the first sentence of the sections to determine the names of the strategies described and thus have an overall picture of what they will be learning about as they read.

A "walk" of any sort can create a basic outline of the upcoming text in the mind of the reader.

The text of this chapter might create a mental outline such as:

I. Reading Strategies

a. Vocabulary

i. Illustrated Dictionary

ii. Four Square

iii. Word Maps

b. Pre-Reading

i. Text/Picture Walk

ii. Predicting

iii. KWL

c. While You are Reading

i. Annotating/Marking the text

ii. Cornell/Two Column Notes/outlining

iii. Metacognitive Awareness

d. Bringing it Home
i. Summarizing/ SPW

iii. Concept Map

iv. ELI5

Another way to begin thinking about the text is predicting. This is one of many strategies that have students connecting with the text. In this case, they are doing so before they get into the reading part. Much of reading is the conversation that one has with the text as they read. It is this conversation that forms understandings, whether we know it is taking place or not. So as a reader approaches a text, predicting can start this conversation with the content intentionally.

The strategy is exactly as it sounds, students look at subject headings and pictures (similarly to a "walk" without the reading of sentences) and they predict what they think they might find out. This serves two basic purposes: 1) They are starting that internal dialogue and 2) They are helping themselves to develop a purpose for reading along with a strategy for their approach. The internal dialogue is something I will focus more in in the "during reading" and "metacognitive" sections, but the purpose for reading and a strategic approach to reading are very important for struggling readers. When readers have a purpose for their reading they can focus on the pieces that they believe will fill in their puzzle. This focus helps students to determine what is important and what us extraneous. One of the difficulties that my struggling readers have is determining what is important. I know that if we do not have a strategy that develops purpose, then those are the readers who will have the most questions and who will likely become overly frustrated. When they have an idea of what to look for and what is not important, their process goes more smoothly and they get what they need in more succinct fashion. The approach that they take is a concentrated metacognitive decision based on the reading strategies that they have for the specific purpose they have in reading. With this in mind, it is important to help students develop and use multiple strategies for reading and also to help them know when to employ those strategies.

The KWL strategy is one that most teachers have heard of or used in their classrooms. In general, it serves the same purposes as the previously described strategies here, but it is useful in the same way, and therefore offers some variety in presentation. The general idea is that students write down what they already know- to activate background knowledge, then what they want to learn or will learn- to give them a purpose for reading or learning, and after they have read or participated in an activity, they write what they have learned-often to summarize.

What I know	What I want to Know	What I learned

I like to modify this slightly with my middle and high school students to give them more direction. As we are often reading for information, but more often researching, I can add different parts to my KWL like "where will I find information," "how will I learn," or "how will I know it is legitimate?" This gives me the KWLHL or KWLWL.

What I know	What I want/need to know	How.Where will I learn it	How will I know my information is legitimate	What I learned

Adding a couple of columns changes up the pace and these can be situationally specific. Taking a strategy that they are already familiar with and making it somewhat more useful and specific to the current subject matter helps students to progress with their metacognitive awareness, as they see how different strategies can be used in multiple ways and can be molded to their specific situation.

Overall, the main goals of any pre-reading strategies are important to mentally preparing readers for their learning and reading experience. As we have them activate their background knowledge and schema, we help students to associate new concepts with what they already know. When readers can make connections and analogies to understandings that they already have, then they can more easily comprehend and retain the new understandings they need. As students develop a purpose for reading and learning, they can focus on the specific things that they need to ascertain from their reading and not focus on the distracting items which can sometimes blur their comprehension. Finally, when struggling readers begin to predict what they think will be coming in the text, they are beginning the very important internal dialogue which good readers have. This connection and communication with self and text draws the reader in and allows the metacognitive awareness of how they are progressing and what they can do to help themselves. The connection to the text that students form with internal dialogue develops a greater association and personal relationship with new learning. In my experience as a language arts, social studies, and science teacher, I found that developing the metacognition and internal dialogue is difficult. I spend a significant amount of time on think alouds which allow my students to see exactly what happens in my mind. As I read out loud and write, students see that I am skilled in both and I explain that they can easily follow similar strategies in order to develop their skills.

While You Are Reading/Learning

The active reading that struggling readers wrestle with can be taught through the use of some specific strategies which engage the internal dialogue which good readers perform as they read. As students are reading for understanding, this internal conversation is somewhat different than it might be while reading fiction. The engagement students have with non-fiction writing as they read for information and understanding can be more difficult for students to develop. The before reading strategies can help to cultivate motivation and purpose, which in combination aid students in their focus, motivation, confidence, and understanding. The approaches students use as they are reading for understanding are pivotal in helping readers glean what they need from the text, keep their thinking and reading organized, maintain focus, and maintain purpose. If students are thinking about what they are reading, how they are processing it, what it means in the grand scheme of their progress, and how it fits into that process/progress, then they are working with metacognitive awareness which will help them to be successful readers and thinkers. The strategy of annotating and marking up the text coupled with some organized note-taking may seem like extra work for students, but some examples and comparisons of their understanding of texts with and without using the strategies should serve to prove through experience that the extra time leads to a more comprehensive understanding of new subject matter.

Students who read non-fiction well often write in the margins and underline or highlight important information. Those students who struggle most often do not approach reading the same way if they have the choice. Hopefully some practice in the finer points of the process will help those who struggle see the benefits of annotations. Marking up text is part of the basic beginnings of teaching that internal conversation that I have been referring to continually. When students have a purpose for reading and a direction to go as they search for new information, annotating text becomes even more precise and useful. As readers work their way through texts for learning related to argumentation, they can be looking for, and marking, multiple items at a time, such as: evidence, legitimacy, reasoning connections, counterargument, data, and anything in between.

The process of annotating a selection of text is simplistic in nature and can be modified to fit any class, purpose, teacher, and student. To annotate a text, the student uses a predetermined set of symbols, words, or anything they would like to indicate different responses to what they are reading. In addition to the symbols, students can write what they are thinking in the margins. Annotating should become personal for each reader and can be a key to the connection to what they are reading that helps so many struggling readers. I encourage my students to develop their own methods for marking up what they read, but I also give them something as a starting off point. I feel it is important to demonstrate and work through some annotating with them. In my demonstrations I focus on helping them to both understand the text and at the same time critically assess what they read.

While students are reading and learning, annotating the text has additional benefits. On the list of symbols is the "&" symbol to indicate something is missing or questionable in nature. This is an area that encourages students to critically assess what they are reading while they are still in the process of forming understandings and learning. Hopefully that part of the process keeps readers from fostering misconceptions while they learn which might take more time later to dispel, or even worse, might lead to completely false knowledge and confidence in that "knowledge."

Annotating Your Internal Conversation

As you read the selection, use the symbols to indicate your thinking about what you are reading. Underline the text and use the appropriate symbol. You can also write in the margins and connections, questions, or realizations you have as you read.

∗ - Something you know is important (you may not know where it fits in yet)

?- you have a question or are confused

!- you are surprised or impacted

&- you think something is missing or questionable in nature

$- motivating factor

+- shows a connection you have personally

E-could be used as evidence

L- indicates a reason to consider something legitimate as evidence or a source

R- Shows a reasoning connection or causation

C- counterargument- indicates this is an alternate point of view

As you read, you can always write your thoughts in the margins! Remember, each time you read something you may be in a different place mentally, emotionally, and with your understanding so you may see it differently each time.

As students practice and make the annotation process more personal, they get better at it. When they use what they have indicated in their annotations to improve their understanding or their argument in general, they will likely come closer to seeing the full benefits and potential that lies within marking up their text. With the specific symbols I have used students can annotate on a computer or on a paper resource.

Another way to help students connect with what they are reading and organize what they are learning as they are trying to comprehend it is two-column notes. These are also often referred to as Cornell notes. In my mind it is similar to outlining, but the terminology and actual practice does not turn student off as much. I make sure at some point during my use of two-column notes, though, that I show the comparison to an outline of the same material so that students can see the further organization that an outline can provide.

I have also been known to go back and forth between the outline view and concept map view of the computer program *Inspiration* to show the similarities of outlines and concept maps. I have received overwhelming support from students for two-column notes throughout my career. Often student carry this idea to other classes as they realize its potential. When I taught math I even used a version of two column notes where students work a problem on one side of the page with each step in the process indicated by a roman numeral. In the opposing column I had them explain what they were doing in each step. The steps in the explanation were labeled with Roman numerals that corresponded to the step that they worked out in the original column. The students then had their own explanation of what they did, had connected the quantitative and qualitative understandings in their heads, and had done the problem as well as the explanation twice.

The basic premise of the two column notes idea is that as a student performs whatever learning activity they are doing, notes are being taken which are organized into two columns. The page is divided into two columns. The column on the left side of the page is for the main ideas in the text. On the right side of the page are the supporting details for that main idea on the left.   Students generally take to this well because it is easy to master. When I introduce the concept of two column notes I often do it in conjunction with a reading selection in their textbook. Without fail, almost every textbook I have ever read has been organized by headings and subheadings that students can use as scaffolds to determine what to put in the left side of their page. I slowly introduce more material that is not organized in

(1) $4 - 6a + \frac{4}{2} = -1 - 5(7 - 2a)$ (1) write the problem

(2) $4 - 6a - 4 = -7(-5(7 - 2a))$ (2) Distribute appropriately for whatever is given

$4 - 6a + \frac{4}{2} = -1 - 35 + 10a$

(3) $4 - 6a + \frac{4}{2} = -7 - 35 + 10a$ (3) Collect like terms on each side of $=$ pay attention to signs

$4 - 2a = -36 + 12a$

(4) $4 - 2a = -36 + 10a$ (4) Perform opposite operations to solve

(5) $4 - 2a + 2a = -36 + 10a + 2a$ (5) Get variables on same side of $=$

$4 = -36 + 12a$ Since $2a$ is subtracted from the left side, add it to both sides to move to other side

(b) $4 + 36 = -36 + 12a + 36$ (b) Since -36 is now added to both sides to move it to other side

$40 = 12a$

(c) $\frac{40}{12} = \frac{12a}{12}$ (c) Since a is divided by 12 will do both sides by 12

$\frac{10}{3} = a$ so the 'a' is isolated

(d) $\frac{10}{3} = a$ (d) put answer in simplest terms

$3\frac{1}{3} = a$

this way, often in the computer lab because material from the internet can be confusing and poorly organized.

Once students have had a bit of practice the concept of organizing their notes and learning as they read, I introduce the idea that they can use the two column approach to organize their argument thinking while they read. Having sections on the left side of their page which correspond to the evidence, data, reasoning, counterargument, and rebuttal pieces of argument allows students to fill in these as they read. In the end, this ends up looking something like the "creating an argument" scaffold that we also use, but it is not a much a spreadsheet style chart as it is notes and organization of those notes. It is a hybrid between the scaffold and the two column notes. I show them a couple of different ways to do this and encourage them, once again, to develop something that works for them. I cannot stress enough how deeply I believe that students will be far more successful if they make the learning strategies their own.

As readers work their way through new learning and understandings, the metacognitive awareness that they have of their process and their collection of strategies is of utmost importance. The idea of metacognitive thinking revolves around the thinker themselves and their knowledge of their personal strategies. The learner must be aware of what methods they are using, perhaps being aware of their critical thinking systems, reading and learning strategies, as well as their level of motivation, and be able to regulate which processes they are using for what purpose. This involves knowing multiple strategies and understanding their situational use. The metacognitive thinker understands what a learning experience calls for in terms of strategies for understanding and approaches the encounter using the appropriate strategy. These thinkers understand that they are a part of the

Before a Claim has been developed (just getting information)	
Fusion	*Occurs on the sun at 15 million K* *On earth currently inefficient* *Requires more energy to start and sustain reaction than we get from the reaction* *Cleaner and more energy than Fission* *Difficult to overcome EM repulsion to fuse atom* *"Natural"*
Fission	*Cleanest and safest form of renewable energy on Earth* *We currently use Fission as a power source* *Currently easier to split an atom than to fuse one* *Fission is safe on Earth as it can be contained and sustained*
Fossil Fuels	*Greenhouse gasses* *Not renewable* *Coal, wood burning,*
Renewable energy	*Wind, hydroelectric, geothermal, nuclear*

After a Claim has been developed (organizing by data/evidence and reasoning points)	
Evidence	-Fusion must occur at 15 million K Once started the yield is 4x as much as fission Magnetic and laser containment require expensive materials and energy (http://www.world-nuclear.org/) No carbon emissions Less waste fuel for the reaction is in lower quantities (http://www.ccfe.ac.uk/introduction.aspx) Requires temps of 15 Million K Must be sustained for long periods (http://hyperphysics.phy-astr.gsu.edu/hbase/nucene/lawson.html#c1)
Reasoning	Requires 15 million K temps Laser and magnetic confinement consume energy and are costly Significant energy production once sustained (http://www2.lbl.gov/abc/wallchart/chapters/14/2.html)
Legitimacy	Data show that the energy produced comes in greater quantities Clean and sustainable energy is preferred for Earth's future Safer – with small mass of fuel, "meltdowns" as with fission are not possible Lockheed is working towards safer and cheaper containment with results expected soon. (http://www.washingtonpost.com/news/capital-business/wp/2014/10/15/nuclear-fusion-energy-in-a-decade-lockheed-martin-is-betting-on-it/) Multiple trusted scientific and government resources Multiple resources corroborating all information No information from just one source
Claim- Fusion is the best hope for sustainable nuclear energy on Earth	

thinking process and as such must be actively engaged in their learning in order to be successful. Metacognitive thinkers also understand that learning itself is a mental process that must be attended to. One who thinks and works metacognitively focuses and concentrates on the task at hand while they are determining the strategies needed to complete that task. Thus, like critical thinking, metacognitive learning and thinking takes more effort and focus than merely copying definitions or answering basic recall questions. The skills required for critical and metacognitive thinking can be taught, but at the same time the learner must remain focused on the task and put forth more effort. As the metacognitive thinker approaches learning, the tasks that they undertake and the thinking which they employ lead to better learning outcomes because in order to work metacognitively, the learner must monitor what they are learning and, more importantly, if they are learning.

The processes that we use to teach our readers effective strategies that they can use for reading, learning, and comprehending are very important with regard to students developing metacognitive awareness. The power to develop this important thought process lies in the think alouds, the scaffolding, and in the communication with our students. During a think aloud, we are giving insight into our own process and thereby our own metacognitive awareness and strategies. We are showing how we monitor our learning and progress. We can speak to our motivation and especially what we do when our motivation is low. As students are scaffolded through different experiences with strategies, personal metacognitive awareness and strategies are emerging within their own consciousness. They realize what works for them in different situations and develop attachments to specific skills, approaches, and tactics.

Communication at all phases of learning is vital. During each phase of learning communicating with our readers to see where they need help, explanation, or just encouragement in and of itself is essential. Think alouds are a way of communicating, but so is general discussion. Students can talk in small groups, pairs, or we can get together as a whole class to see what everyone is feeling about working with new and different approaches or using tried and true schemes. Students need to opportunity to express themselves and at the same time they need to hear what other students are thinking and feeling as they learn to monitor their own learning and motivation. I cannot think of a time when hearing what helps someone else to stay motivated or connect with a strategy has not helped at least one person in the class. As long as they are getting something out of the discussions, I always try to make time to have them. Whether students benefit from expressing or listening during the talks, they are always helpful.

The art of journaling is another communication method readers can use in order to practice metacognitive awareness.   Journaling motivates students to connect with their thinking in a way that discussion does not. Because students are writing down their personal thoughts and connections, they are also becoming more aware of their processes. At the same time, journaling shows readers that their thoughts are important to what they are doing and that the overall experience is their own. When students write down their thoughts they tend to organize those thoughts more effectively and hopefully dig a little deeper to totally understanding their approach to learning and to each strategy that they journal about using. It is essentially their personal version of a think aloud. Explaining what they are thinking about, just like explaining what they are learning, helps students to fully understand it. The collection of students' journals gives them a record of the effectiveness of the strategy and also another reminder of the strategies themselves.

After Learning Strategies

When students have completed their reading and research it is time for them to ensure they understand the subject matter, their understanding is organized, shore up their memory, and find the holes in their comprehension. Post reading approaches often focus on recounting and organizing information attained from the text. The three strategies that I use the most in this arena are summarizing, concept maps, and *Explain it to Me Like I'm 5*, or ELI5.

Summarizing is a technique that is intrinsic to reading and understanding. Textbooks are built on the premise of summarizing a vast ocean of knowledge and making it approachable for students. Students who have read a significant amount of text and used some of the "during reading" strategies should be able to produce a summary of what the text was about. I do not just have students summarize, though. Many students do not come to me with the ability to actually summarize what they have read or learned. In general, I get a full scale retelling of what they have read. This is not very helpful in many cases. Regurgitating information does not mean that a reader has understood or comprehended that information. With that in mind, I use some specific summarizing strategies which help students to get to the heart of what they have read.

One of these strategies is Sentence-Phrase-Word, or SPW. This approach works best with text of 2-3 pages. In this system, students read the text with the goal of distilling the meaning of the text by choosing a sentence, a phrase, and a single word that are most important according to that student. This idea focuses the reader on a sentence that truly sums up the heart of the reading. I tell my students that this is the overall thesis statement or what we are truly supposed to get from the reading. At the same time, a key phrase is chosen as well. Often writers have tendencies to a certain phrase, especially when that phrase is integral to the topic or subject matter. The phrase piece also allows students to further support their sentence or bring in secondary ideas to the summary. The final piece is the single word component. This can be especially challenging to students. In order to choose the most important word they must truly understand the ultimate focus of the text. I have seen students debate internally for as long as I would give them to choose their word. The fact that they were not satisfied and that they continued that internal dialogue proved to me that the strategy worked well. Readers that are successful in these three choices understand what they have read thoroughly. A quick venture around the room in which everyone gives their sentence, then phrase, and finally their words allows everyone to see the text from multiple points of view. This differentiation in viewpoints adds to their practice at critical thinking and assessment as well.

SPW

SENTENCE-PHRASE-WORD

Read the Selection Thoroughly

When you have completed the reading, choose:

A sentence that you think sums up the meaning of the selection

Then when he exited the car and touched the gas pump nozzle, the electricity sparked and ignited the gas fumes coming from his car's gas tank.

A phrase that you feel is important to your understanding

people touch them, their bodies discharge static

The most important word from the selection

Static

Little-known dangers at gas pumps

From Elizabeth Cohen

ATLANTA, Georgia (CNN) --Few American motorists know that static electricity around gas pumps can ignite a deadly fire.

Ignacio Sierra has personal experience of that danger. He was pumping gasoline when his vehicle suddenly burst into flames with his daughter Esperanza inside.

"She started screaming," remembers Sierra. "I knew if I opened the door, the flames would start to go inside."

He did manage to get Esperanza out unharmed, but the fire ruined his car and destroyed the gas station.

Sierra set off the blaze by doing something many motorists do; he re-entered his car to retrieve money while the gas was still pumping.

His movement created friction against the car seat that built up static electricity in his body. Then when he exited the car and touched the gas pump nozzle, the electricity sparked and ignited the gas fumes coming from his car's gas tank.

About a dozen victims of static gas pump fires have talked to CNN. All said they had no idea this sort of fire was a possibility until it happened to them. And some say they will never put gas in their vehicles if their children are with them.

A woman who asked to be identified only as Carol said a static gas pump fire is blamed for burning her daughter so badly she needed skin grafts on her legs.

Carol had put the gas pump nozzle on automatic and re-entered her car to write a check. When her then-12-year-old daughter, wearing a sweater and jacket that may have created static electricity, reached for the nozzle, flames suddenly ignited her clothing.

The Petroleum Equipment Institute (PEI) has documented 129 such fires since the early 1990s.

All those fires infuriate electrical engineer Steven Fowler because he says they were all preventable.

"We have to accept the fact that refueling is dangerous. We can't hide that from the public anymore," said Fowler, a static electricity expert.

The solution, he said, is to put up stickers that read "touch me." The stickers are placed over metal and when people touch them, their bodies discharge static electricity safely.

But Fowler said no gas stations plan to put them up, except for the SPINX Oil Company chain of 80 stations in South Carolina.

The American Petroleum Institute is concerned that those stickers may detract from other warnings such as ones about smoking while pumping gas, which is far more dangerous.

"That whole debate is what is the right language and how do we best warn our customers how do they safely refill?" said Denise McCourt of the American Petroleum Institute.

Some stations do put up a list of warnings, which include static fires, but Fowler said the advice gets lost in a sea of words.

However, consumers need to be warned of another fire danger involving gas pump nozzles, according to Fowler.

A surveillance videotape from a gas station in Oklahoma shows a fire that cost the life of a 32-year-old mother of four. It's not known what caused the fire, but had the woman left the nozzle in the gas tank, engineers say she probably would have lived.

But the nozzle was too hot, Fowler said, so the woman grabbed the hose.

"When she did, it did a snake routine and sprayed gasoline in all directions and she tried to get away but it was too late," he said.

Again, only one gasoline chain in South Carolina plans on using labels on nozzles that warn: In case of fire, do not remove nozzle from the vehicle.

"We have seen the film of that woman that actually died. And we don't want that to happen," said Eric Baumholser of SPINX.

But the American Petroleum Institute says just reading the label could be dangerous.

"We probably don't want to have people have their face that close to that nozzle," said McCourt.

Find this article at:

http://www.cnn.com/2002/US/12/05/gas.pump.fires/index.html?eref= sitesearch

The idea of a concept map can go along with some during reading strategies. However, it can be an activity that allows students to organize fully what they have learned. At the same time, it can be used to fuse understandings taken across multiple texts or an entire research session. As a teacher who can struggle at times to differentiate for more artistic students, I enjoy the concept map because of its visual qualities. With the concept map, students can absolutely use illustrations or even pictures to complete the connections. Having the artistic students apply themselves with this strategy is often a relief for them. Many students like drawing pictures as opposed to writing when we have been writing more often during a unit. They quickly realize, though, that using pictures as representations on their concept maps becomes similar to summarizing and organizing at the same time. It is a good exercise of all students to do both at the same time. It is definitely a higher cognitive activity when it is done that way.

Oceanic Invertebrate Concept Map

After reading the packet on Oceanic Invertebrates, organize the information into the concept map

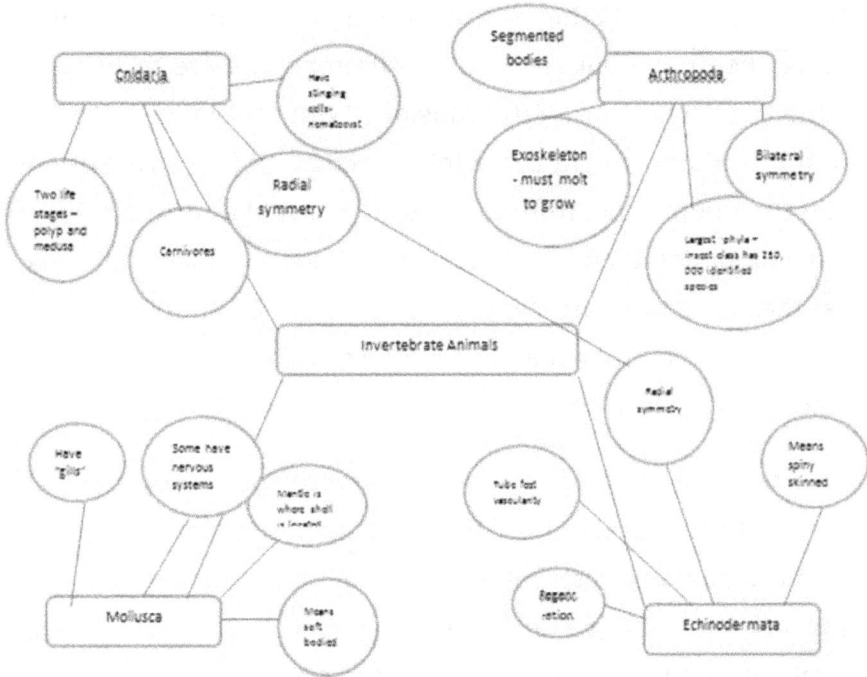

As has been explained previously, the concept map organizes the information into the ways in which it is connected overall. A concept map allows the reader to see all of the connections visually rather than just mentally or in text from. The thinking that goes into making the concept map encourages students to fortify their understandings and to see the intricacies of what they are reading and learning. A great benefit is seeing new connections as students create the maps and making connections across multiple texts. Seeing similar or corroborating ideas across different resources contributes to the idea of legitimacy of information. At the same time, student may also notice contradictions in ideas across multiple texts, which should have them questioning the legitimacy of information...or at least taking a closer look at the sources or their ideas.

One of my favorite things to say to students as they are creating arguments is for them to do all of the thinking for their reader. Often I can be heard saying things like, "Imagine your reader has never heard of your subject," or "Pretend you are talking to a child in elementary school or a little cousin." With that in mind, the after reading technique of ELI5 came into practice. When a reader has to explain the information from the text in words that a small child of five years could understand, they must thoroughly explain what they read and at the same time use easy simple words. Often, this leads them to realize that they may not fully understand the vocabulary used in the text, or that they need a quick re-read of what they have learned.

For students to use the simplest language to talk about the ideas from the text they must truly understand it and have internalized it. This is also a perfect strategy to have a bit of fun with. I did not necessarily know that when I started using it, but my students quickly determined that it was the case. I often use this strategy to lighten up dull or especially somber topics. Having a bit of fun with this strategy is great, because it can truly be difficult for students if they need to go back to the text multiple times as they realize their understanding and grasp of the material is not what they thought it was. I generally have students perform ELI5 in pairs and then as a class we can decide on the best one, the most informative, or sometimes, the most amusing.

ELI5

After reading the selection, explain the main points and ideas as if you were talking to a young child of elementary school age.

Solar cells work by changing the sun's light energy into the electric energy that we use to power things that plug in or use batteries. Photons from the sun are pieces of light that are like particles. Things called semi-conductors have the ability to take the energy from the sun's photons and use it to cause other pieces of energy called electrons to move and create their energy. The best semi-conductor to use in solar panels is called silicon. Once the electrons start moving, they move like they are going downhill from silicon pieces that have too many electrons to silicon pieces that have too few of the electrons. The electrons move like this to even out the solar panel. The movement of these electrons is what gives us electrical energy that we use in our devices.

How do solar cells work? (www.physics.org)

Solar (or photovoltaic) cells convert the sun's energy into electricity. Whether they're adorning your calculator or orbiting our planet on satellites, they rely on the photoelectric effect: the ability of matter to emit electrons when a light is shone on it.

Silicon is what is known as a semi-conductor, meaning that it shares some of the properties of metals and some of those of an electrical insulator, making it a key ingredient in solar cells. Let's take a closer look at what happens when the sun shines onto a solar cell.

Sunlight is composed of miniscule particles called photons, which radiate from the sun. As these hit the silicon atoms of the solar cell, they transfer their energy to loose electrons, knocking them clean off the atoms. The photons could be compared to the white ball in a game of pool, which passes on its energy to the colored balls it strikes.

Freeing up electrons is however only half the work of a solar cell: it then needs to herd these stray electrons into an electric current. This involves creating an electrical imbalance within the cell, which acts a bit like a slope down which the electrons will flow in the same direction.

Creating this imbalance is made possible by the internal organization of silicon. Silicon atoms are arranged together in a tightly bound structure. By squeezing small quantities of other elements into this structure, two different types of silicon are created: n-type, which has spare electrons, and p-type, which is missing electrons, leaving 'holes' in their place.

When these two materials are placed side by side inside a solar cell, the n-type silicon's spare electrons jump over to fill the gaps in the p-type silicon. This means that the n-type silicon becomes positively charged, and the p-type silicon is negatively charged, creating an electric field across the cell. Because silicon is a semi-conductor, it can act like an insulator, maintaining this imbalance.

As the photons smash the electrons off the silicon atoms, this field drives them along in an orderly manner, providing the electric current to power calculators, satellites and everything in between.

Once again, this was not intended to be an exhaustive venture into reading and vocabulary strategies. However, both researching and creating arguments are literacy heavy and I felt as though some strategic help was warranted here. I tried to give three strategies to help with each stage of reading processes. There are many others that are beneficial and are favorites of colleagues. These are mostly my favorite approaches to helping my struggling readers.

Chapter 7: Some Parting Thoughts

"We do not learn from experience... we learn from reflecting on experience."

— John Dewey

I sincerely hope that this volume has filled you with as much hope and excitement as it has me. During the many phases of the studies and teaching that have brought me to this point, I have developed a deeper love for what I do and much more hope for the future of my students and for the future of education in general than I had even when I was a new bright eyed teacher fresh into the classroom. There is no one who has known me for a significant amount of time that does not realize I sincerely believe what I have been telling you here is something that could truly revolutionize and propel education in the United States to an unparalleled level of greatness. I say this because scientific argumentation, along the practices that accompany it, has been proven through research and experience to be effective at training and developing better and more effective thinkers. The ideas and concepts held as the basis for the argumentation process are time tested. This is not a passing fad. As far back as ancient thinkers have existed, intelligent people have created understanding and developed knowledge in this manner. Some of the great thinkers that we teach about in school, emulate as famously successful minds, and fashion as pillars of renowned and celebrated past societies have discovered, molded, and made significant use of scientific argumentation. I support this specifically because it is not merely a way of teaching or simply a process that you can put into your teaching rotation as a method you use from time to time; this is a way of thinking that is to be woven throughout your classes, your students, their scholastic endeavors, and most importantly, their lives. It is time to teach students to think once again. The critical thinking skills and metacognitive awareness that I have seen in my students after mere months into the process still amazes me each time I get a new group and work with them in this manner.

Something about myself that I noticed well into my collegiate career (likely would have come earlier if I had much interested in someone else educating me rather than having to do everything myself) was that it is through writing that I truly develop my thinking and understanding of what I am working to figure out. When we write we must think about what we are saying and what ideas, either our own or those we are emulating, are going into our language. It is necessary to think about all that we have done leading up to the moment of writing. The research, the thinking, the discussions, the practice, the metacognitive awareness, and all other parts of the process come together as one when we write about it. As we craft out ideas, they become clearer and they develop even further. Through the development of this volume I found even more clarity about scientific argumentation, even after the many years that I have been working within the concept in and outside of my classroom. I developed new ideas for implementation and different ways to approach teaching argumentation. I truly write to focus and to clear my head. If I recall, people in the industry call this "writing to learn." Even as I heard such terminology, I never truly grasped the concept for my own personal use. Clearly, I was not metacognitively aware. Essentially, I learned about what works for me by doing things. I learned by trying something and focusing on what I was doing. I am pretty sure that I was only as focused as I was because of my level of interest. I truly believe that if we want our students to learn, we must develop some level of interest or intrinsic motivation. This can be difficult, but there is a way, if we have faith.

If we trust that the learning our students will do will be more effective and more sincere with greater focus and retention, then we have time to do the training for this learning on the front end. I know every teacher feels as though they are under the gun and that their time is limited. I have said this myself many times, but there are times that are we are doing less important things and there are days that are not as productive as they could be. So if we just substitute those days that are a bit off target and those days that everyone is not into it, with days that are frontloading technique, then we stay on track. I reiterate that this is work and will not be easy. This is a change in thinking and the way in which we teach. However, it has been proven time and time again through research...peer reviewed research...my own research and experience to be AT LEAST as effective as other teaching and more often far more effective in the ways that matter. Students who practice scientific argumentation in ANY classroom or subject are helping to make themselves better students in general and more effective thinkers. These skills will serve them in the classroom and in the world. So to create those skills, to create that intrinsic motivation, and to create interest in content as well as the process, we will have to have faith.

The implementation of socio-scientific topics during the skill development part of scientific argumentation will help students to realize the benefits of the process and the focus that they need when researching. The motivation will already be there if they are working with something that they are already interested in. They are more likely to perform the tasks necessary to develop skills and be more focused all the while with their own topics at hand. In the beginning, this is absolutely necessary. It is not, I repeat, it is absolutely not a waste of time at all. Through the development of the skills and the success students have in creating an understanding that is likely unmatched previously in their experience, you as the teacher have the high ground when you point out the skills they are developing and the effectiveness of the process. It also allows you to specifically refer to their focus as a determining factor at the same time as their practice of the scientific argumentation methodologies. Socio-scientific topics give the students a greater ability to find information, have some amount of background understandings, use their own assertions regarding topics, be able to spot evidence that is devoid of truth or expertise, develop their reasoning skills and patterns, and spot the holes in counterargument evidence and reasoning patterns. Overall research shows that students do better when using topics that contain some sort of social consciousness and content. This can be done as a run through of the full process at the beginning of the year. It is possible to use the scaffolds and create a full argument in groups at the beginning of the school year. This can be a team building activity and a way for students to get to know each other. Once students experience the success of this event, it is time to go through the protocol for teaching and mastering the specific steps as detailed previously. I am sure you have realized through this volume that there are countless ways to implement these methods. I am sure that as you read every section your mind was bursting with ways to interlace scientific argumentation into your tried and true teaching strategies and lesson plans. I know every time I write about it I do the same thing. The best ways to get started is to just get started.

Try it one or two times. Spend a week or two of your summer or winter break and see what you think you can do. It works. Just make sure you are ready when you do it, because there will be questions, you will be busy helping students constantly, and you will have to understand what I have written here thoroughly. You are a professional and an artist in your field. You can do it because you know yourself and you will know your students better than anyone. Make it happen. This is a great way to develop relationships among your students and between you and your students. Enjoy!

AFTERWORD – Other Educational Movements

As an educator, it feels as though every 3-5 years, there is a new "hot" idea that is going to save education or that is going to help teach students in new and better ways. However many of the driving forces for these movements are not new and are not based in science or research.

The ideologies behind these reforms can be placed in to three basic categories as outlined by Labaree (1997, 2011) and Pennycook (2011): democratic education, social efficiency, and social mobility. Education in America itself from its early incarnations could be linked in many ways to the public good. With a new country and a new democracy, even the founding fathers understood it was important to educate those who would live and serve therein. Education could be seen as a way to preserve the democracy and have the citizenry sufficiently educated to perform that tasks which were expected of them. This driving idea would lead to perhaps the first major education reform... the idea that education should be for all citizens. Significant reforms would revolve around the idea of social efficiency. As the capitalist economy expanded exponentially, the idea that workers needed specific skills to drive that economy led to the greater institution of public education and the inclusion of a more significant portion of the population. Reforms in the realm of social efficiency were driven by employers and job creators, thus their ideologies and needs drove the reform and the curriculum. In the more modern era, the idea of equality in education and education as a form of social mobility drove reform ideologies. Pennycook (2011) notes that efforts at social reform through the education system are political, not educational, in nature. It is these modern reform efforts that often lead away from a focus on educational success and enter the realm of politics, where the greater good of the student may not always be at the forefront of the ideological pressure.

In order to examine this further, let's take a look at some current movements and ideological approaches in education. This is not meant to be an exhaustive examination, but merely a snapshot of some basic movements in the field.

Standards Based Education Movement

The standards based movement in education could be described as being born out of a lack of accountability across the educational industry as a whole. Out of the 1986 National Governor's Association meeting came a desire not only for heightened educational outcomes, but an impetus on grand overarching standards to inform the individual state and local standards. Along with these new standards was also a shift from an input orientation to an outcome orientation (Murnane & Levy, 2001). In theory, with a greater specificity regarding what is to be taught, there could be a more positive outcome for the student, their learning, and their achievement. Through some specific research on the statistics regarding those outcomes, Carbonaro & Covay (2010) denote that the standards being more specific with a focus on what is to be learned have indeed improved scores on the standardized tests designed to measure the aforementioned outcomes. Also, according to research by Costrell & Betts (2001), standards have led to improvements in teacher action and student effort. Along with the increased focus on defining the standards also came frameworks and materials to help with the attainment of those standards. It is difficult to disagree with an attempt to make one of the more difficult parts of educational theory, the question of what to teach, as clear and concise as possible.

With the effort to clearly define the standards also came certain poignant criticisms. One of the greatest criticisms centered on the reduction in autonomy for the state and local governments. Education had always been under the foray of the local systems until the implementations of the ESEA and the Title I funding. However, even with procedural influence, the standards based movement began an approach that looked to inform the subject matter to be taught as well. Along with the loss of autonomy also came an even greater dependence on outside entities, such as textbook companies, curriculum companies, testing companies, and others writing and planning for the standards (Costrell & Betts, 2001). In many cases, certain companies could be responsible for influencing the standards and then selling the materials to assist in understanding and teaching those same standards. Control seemed to be shifting from the public entities of local government and school systems more and more to private industries.

The standards themselves created the problem of fully understanding, interpreting, and transferring the new standards into the classroom. The intricacies of expectations, especially at the high level that seemed to be the focus of the general movement, could present issues, as educators were often not involved with the actual writing of the standards. Perhaps the greatest backlash of the standards based educational movement came from that lack of influence from educational professionals on the actual authorship of the standards. However, the most significant issue with most educational reform movements is the lack of input from industry professionals involved in the actual teaching of students.

An offshoot of the standards based movement is the standards based grading ideology that has started to accompany the concept. The idea there centers on grading the mastery of the standard only. The idea is that students should be graded and should be held accountable for the mastery of the standard only. With this comes an ideological shift away from the preparation of students for citizenship and the workforce and solely to the basis of whether the identified standard has been taught and learning has been acquired. Therefore, grades would indicate only a qualitative statement as to if the standard had been mastered, not mastered, or was still in progress. Not as a numerical, quantitative score.   This does not leave the grades completely open to qualitative assessment, though, as much of what goes into the grade is still quantitative in nature. There must be legitimate proof that the standard was mastered. In this vein, everything must be labeled with the standard it is associated with.

The idea of standards based grading leads to a focus on data and how it can be used. There is no reason to spend more time than necessary in standards that students already know, just because it is in the curriculum and has always been taught in a certain way. Mining the data from both formative and summative assessments can help teachers to plan more effective lessons targeting specifically what needs to be taught, reinforced, or remediated. Also, students are aware very specifically of what they are being assessed on. The standards are clear and so is the method of assessment. Standards based grading could help to revolutionize the way students are promoted within tracks of education and core areas. Much of the basis for how we promote students could change with a standards based grading reform initiative that takes hold and influences those who structure school systems.

One of the staunchest criticisms of standard based grading is the loss of the hidden curriculum and its significant contribution as a part of the education of individuals capable of living in a society. Essentials to daily life as a citizen such as: performing tasks in a timely manner, taking responsibility for task performance in a correct manner the first time or when necessary, budgeting time, time management, personal responsibility in general, and intrinsic motivation are not consistently a part of student educations. Not only is this a different direction from many other reform movements, but it seems to be in direct opposition to democratic or citizenry education and social mobility education. With regards to holistically educating a student, standards based grading has little influence or appeal. Many opponents of standards based grading imply that it benefits lazy or unmotivated students to the detriment of those who need structure and assistance with responsibility. Allowing students to turn in assignments whenever they complete them as long as they master the content by the end of the grading period does not teach many of the personal responsibility pieces of a life as a productive member of society. This is perhaps the greatest criticism of standards based grading. There must surely be some middle ground in the matter that could combine the good points of a less quantitative measurement of student success which is not to the detriment of basic life skills.

No Child Left Behind

The most significant movement regarding standards based education and accountability is the legislation signed into law by George W. Bush in 2001, No Child left Behind (NCLB). Beginning with the first incarnation of the Elementary and Secondary Education Act (ESEA) under the Johnson administration, a new approach to schooling and accountability began. Until that point, the responsibility for the education of the American school child fell solely on the individual state. Constitutionally, the federal government had no power or authority in the matter. With the ESEA, however, came a particular entity known as Title I of that act. With Title I, the federal government began to dole out financial aid to states. Soon it was discovered that with that financial benefit also came the looming eye of the government and the hand would soon rock the cradle. There are almost always strings attached to federal financial benefits. Those strings rose to a heighted level with the 2001 reauthorization of ESEA, also known as No Child Left Behind (NCLB). With this law, the federal government took an unprecedented role in the education of public school children across the nation. The only power they wielded was money under Title I of the law. The goal of NCLB was purported to be accountability and equality in education for all students, especially focused on the closing of achievement gaps amongst special populations.

Perhaps the most significant cause of uproar amongst those in the educational industry and parents alike might be the "accountability" movement attached to NCLB and the high stakes testing to which it is connected. As an educator who was in the industry during the transition to the NCLB mindset, I can say there are both good and bad effects within the movement. A major impetus of the NCLB legislation was the idea of accountability in association with the standard of education that the law was striving for. All other things aside, accountability in and of itself is not a bad idea. Superfine (2004) points out that many systems already had high stakes tests determining student overall outcomes and tying scores to promotion, graduation, and other scholastic decisions regarding the students themselves. The tests were tied to the individual students and their performance determined their outcomes. With NCLB, however, came newly applied pressure and accountability for the entire building, district, system, and state based on the prosperity of the students' tests. This extra pressure and accountability was suddenly displaced from the students and applied to other entities. Although the students did still depend greatly on their performance for promotion and progress, those scores were now used to hold teachers and systems accountable for what was purported to be student achievement.

In theory, this does not sound like a bad idea. The law itself sought to develop a greater educational experience for many groups that were previously underrepresented in the minds of school administrators, educational planners, and often the general public. The large scale implementation of inclusion programs for special education students as well as English Language Learners came about as the idea of the least restrictive environment for students gained traction. At the time that many of the ideas were being implemented, I was a teacher involved with English Language Learners, or ELL, students. In many cases, there was little or no accountability for the educational practices use in ELL classrooms. These students did not have to take the same tests as the other students and I believe because of this, their education suffered. With the students and the teachers held accountable the level of education definitely improved. Students were no longer in self-contained ELL classrooms; instead they were in the regular classroom learning the same things as every other student. With NCLB all students were expected to achieve. Once again though, the only methodology was testing and holding teachers accountable. It was up to teachers to perform what would amount to reforming education with no true direction from those who would be holding them accountable and no money to pay for such a revolution.

In the grand scheme of raising levels of performance and closing achievement gaps, the fact that every child was supposed to achieve at the same level did lead to more students having access to the same education as others. At the same time, this led to greater achievement and the narrowing of many achievement gaps. However, the lack of a true direction and the funding necessary to fix what had now been identified as needing to be fixed left educators struggling and longing for the "good old days."

Once again, this seems like a good idea and steps in the right direction have come from the accountability movement. However, I do not sense an underlying epistemological belief or structure directing what is important or how learning takes place. That is left up to the teachers in the classroom. There is no "heart" in the movement. The central idea is that all students should have access to the same education. That is wonderful. There is no true methodology. There are standards to be met which are represented by test scores. No one is suggesting how to get things done other than to say everyone deserves the same basic education. With that ideology at the center of the proposed movement, there is the likelihood that in our capitalist society, the path of least resistance will be the one taken. Even educators who put their heart and soul into their work on a daily basis may be forced to take the "easy "road. When there are standards suggesting that too much information and too many concepts must be taught, the pawns that are successful in this game are those that can determine what is on the test and teach those items more intensely. At times this is to the detriment of fluidity or connecting concepts naturally. Some items which are important to a full understanding can be left out for the sake of time. This is what happens when there is a test or a standard navigating educational practices, rather than a sound scientifically based principle.

Academic Rigor

Also from the standards based movement, emerges questions of academic rigor. The desire to institute rigor into the curriculum could be considered a direct response to the criticism of NCLB and the newly developed high stakes tests. The criticism involved the idea that teachers were "teaching to the test" and that students were merely learning what was purported to be on the tests with little regard to how it connects to other information and ideas or how it fits into a bigger educational picture. The days of creating the "renaissance student" had been over for some time, and issues were beginning to arise. Some suggest that as the states and systems are responsible for the assessment of the students, the nature of the tests themselves and their academic rigor come into question. In the grand scheme of things, once again, it is the students who get lost and pay the price for political posturing and clamoring for control of the tax revenue flooding into the school systems.

The idea of adding academic rigor to the curriculum often revolves around the concepts laid out in Bloom's Taxonomy or some derivative. In general, students are asked to do more than just recall information. With a rigorous academic curriculum, students are expected to manipulate and apply the information they have acquired. The application is assumed to be associated with new situations. Students are generally asked to synthesize multiple pieces of information or sources and at times, are asked to create something with what they have learned. There is no problem at all with these expectations, as these processes are absolutely something all people have to do in life either periodically or on a consistent basis. As with many other reforms, in theory this is a positive step. More thinking and the application of understanding acquired is rigorous and should help produce better thinkers and, as such, stronger minds.

Examining the rigor movement from the position of teachers and students however, can lead to some negative effects, responses, and outcomes. First, a major criticism comes from the point of view of the student. If the major gauge of their performance is a test, in general teachers have been conditioned to essentially teach what they think will be on the test, and that test has generally been recall and perhaps little more, then it does not seem to be in their best interest to learn a new way. In the same vein, if the idea of rigor is something that is being implemented from the top down, i.e. the test designers are putting in higher level thinking questions which require a rigorous and thorough understanding of the curriculum, how is that fair to students who have been taught in a different way for what could amount to their entire scholastic careers? This mismatch makes the test itself invalid. If this is the desire of the powers that be in education, then this must be a process. There has to be a plan and steps toward the fruition of that plan. Teachers need to develop new lessons and new ways of teaching that will meet the new requirements. The consistent "shocking" of the educational system every decade or so cannot continue. The desire for rigor is not the issue. As it is often the case, approaching the idea with no central ideology which is accepted by teachers and students is the issue.

Project Based Learning

Project based learning is a furtherance of the idea of inquiry based learning relating back to progressive education ideas from the turn of the 20th century. Dewey (1903, 1938) espoused the idea that students would receive a more authentic education which would be more applicable to the world around them if they concentrated on tasks and activities which emulated the world in which they lived along with the expectations for inclusion in that world. In addition, students would show more motivation and interest in what they were learning if they saw how it fit into preparation for the real world. Students having some say in their inquiry lessons also should lead to better work and more astute outcomes. Dewey's research supported these ideals. Project based learning is a modern effort to develop a usable educational approach for the current era that uses these principles and develops processes to teach and evaluate academic success. In the sea of educational reform, project based learning, or PBL, has a basis in a succinct ideology and research. There is a clear focus and a record of success in the field of inquiry based education.

A common definition of PBL along with basic criteria can be found through the Buck Learning Institute and through the assemblage of literature from Thomas (2000). The benefits if PBL are also seen in the basic premises which guide and define these projects. Benefits to a PBL curricular design include authenticity, student involvement, student voice, applied learning, academic rigor, active exploration, and the facilitation of communication skills with both peers and adults (Bell, 2010; Lattimer & Riordan, 2011; Tamin & Grant, 2013). Research has shown that students do achieve better outcomes and higher scores on the standardized tests design to measure their educational outcomes (Hovey & Ferguson, 2014). With a PBL model at least some of this success can be attributed to the improvement in motivation in both teachers and students. As teachers and students explore the curriculum through more interesting and relative ways

their level of intrinsic motivation should rise. With the rise in teachers'
motivations, even if it is only a perceived rise in motivations, comes a
rise in students' motivations leading to more attentive and successful
work (Lam, Cheng, &Ma, 2009).

Tamim & Grant (2013) showed that critical thinking skills
improved through the PBL process as students were involved in
constructivist investigations. This lends itself to their position
describing PBL as a constructivist approach to learning. The
constructivist epistemological stance describes a method of learning in
which knowledge is created through active engagement and
exploration. This is different from the traditional scenario in which
students listen and learn what has already been determined to be
knowledge. In a constructivist approach, the student is at the center
of creating and processing the understanding that will become their
knowledge base. PBL learning at its core is a representation of
constructivist education as described. Students are helping to direct
their learning and are pursuing their educational goals independently
during many points in the PBL process. Within the search for answers
and explanations for the problems decided on (often by students
through some direction from teachers), students are creating their
own education and at the same time their own new knowledge.
Through critically examining the materials available, students are
developing new (to them) ideas and innovations for solving their
problems. This is a genuine example of critical thinking.

PBL also allows for the integration of the curriculum, another
area of research involving scholastic reform. Beane (1997) describes
curriculum integration as a process that focuses the general curriculum
in all of its facets around a central problem. This is essentially the

heart of the PBL movement as well. The curriculum integration movement seeks to do many of the same things as the PBL movement, yet it is sometimes seen as different in nature. The curriculum integration model also has been described as a thematic education where grand themes are taught through everything that goes into them (Pate, Homestead, &McGinnis, 1997). Also within that definition comes a parallel to, and direct correlation with, the original middle school movement of the late 1960's and early 1970's, which was born out of the issues with the junior high model. As junior high schools were showing that treating middle grades children like they were small high school students was not working, the idea that they should be taught in a special way was born. Within this model, which took special consideration to development levels corresponding to social and emotional changes within these students, also came the idea that they should be approaching learning in a different way. It was theorized that students should learn content through relationship between information and not through the traditional subject area separations (Eichhorn, 1969, 1973). As the separation between the subjects seemed unnatural, it made more sense to teach through an integrated curriculum in which students solved thematically based problems and sorted through real world issues to develop the knowledge and understandings expected of them. Although made more popular by the development of the middle school model and examined as a special way to teach special students, it is clear that this was not a fully new idea and could be applied to the general school population. The current PBL movement has built on the past incarnations of problem based learning and its impetus of curriculum integration has begun to make good use of this ideology in the modern school reform era.

With the good of PBL, even with its rich history of theoretical and actual success, also come issues as teachers attempt to apply the ideas in the modern school. As teachers are pulled far out of their comfort zone and out of a strictly designed and often already laid out curriculum, it can be difficult to shift into new territory. It requires a "leap of faith" by teaches as they are working in different ways in order to achieve new and better outcomes (Lee, Blackwell, Drake, & Moran, 2014). However, the students must still be measured by the same standardized tests as other students. The step towards PBL Education takes a shift in the ideologies and methodologies of these teachers, often going against the ways they were educated and trained to teach. Accepting and working within a constructivist approach to teaching and learning is in direct opposition to general teacher training. The movement towards a student centered and student driven process can be a struggle for teachers. Nervousness and a lack of complete direction can make teachers less motivated and sometimes confused. With the motivation of teachers being a pivotal point in the process, this can lead to issues.

In addition to the struggles that teachers have in assimilating to a very new idea of teaching, students have similar struggles working within a distinctly different realm of learning. Self-regulated learning (SRL) is a point of issue for many students (English & Kitsantas, 2013). The idea that the students themselves are responsible for planning their time, using their time wisely and appropriately, as well as developing a plan for working within the problem or project that they are facing can be a tough idea to get used to. The intensity of the group work that student need to do is also difficult for many. Students must make and maintain relationships with those they work with in order to be successful (Latimore &

Riordan, 2011). In the traditional classroom, the individual student is generally responsible for themselves and for their learning only. The need to depend on others can be difficult to get used to. A sincere problem for many students also comes from the fact that in order to make true progress they need to struggle with the content, the major concepts, and the problem that they are working on (Tamim & Grant, 2013). Students have been indoctrinated to believe struggling with information is the road to failure and that if they are not learning quickly they may not be successful. Actively struggling with concepts is seen as a failure on the part of the student. Just as teachers must make that "leap of faith," so must the students.

Perhaps the strongest points of opposition for PBL are the issues relating the system wide standards to projects and problems that are coherent and cohesive. In addition to the curriculum matching, the timetables set by the state and individual school systems for their testing schedules may not align with the timelines of projects and knowledge acquisition (Tamim & Grant, 2013). Working out the minutia of relating standards and timetables to a completely new way of teaching and learning can be very stressful for teachers. Teachers must also design these projects in a way that all of the content is incorporated. With that in mind, there are levels of expertise that many teachers do not possess (Tamim & Grant, 2013). It is difficult for teachers to see across multiple curricular areas when they were trained to implement a specific subject matter and content. With the difficulties in designing and implementing projects, also come the issues with assessment. As PBL teaching is very different, so is the assessment of the final product delivered. The process itself must be examined, but the final product is immensely important, too. The assessment of PBL projects requires a realignment in ideology and practice for teachers who choose to implement this style of teaching and learning. Overall, with the issues that can be encountered by both teachers and students, research has shown that the unknown is not so much a question anymore. Research has clearly shown PBL to work well with many different kinds of learners (Lam et al., 2009; Bell, 2010; Hovey & Ferguson, 2014).

Common Core

Common core has appeared at a time when the desire for an equal educational experience for all seems to be at a high point. It was born out of a disenfranchisement with NCLB and the standards that came along with it. Although there are polarizing opinions representing multiple points of view regarding common core, it is deceptively basic in its premise and design. At its heart, the common core is merely a set of standards which are adopted by the educational systems of states within the US. Currently, the number of states having adopted these standards is 45. Delving deeper, there is more to the picture, though.

The reactionary piece of the common core standards comes in direct opposition to the perceived decline of educational standards under the NCLB legislation. Under NCLB and previous systems, states were able to make standards which were specialized for their local systems and were meant to meet only the perceived needs of those localities. The common core standards have been designed to be rigorous and challenging for all students in a purposeful way to develop equality on the outcomes of public education (Kornhaber, Griffith, & Tyler, 2014). Overall, the operative word in the title is "common." Many believe that for there to be true equality in educational opportunities, there must be true equality in the education provided. Common standards across the board for these 45 states that have adopted these ideas mean that the students in the schools are coming closer to a standardized scholastic experience. The ideology follows the previously mentioned push for equality in outcomes with a desire to close the achievement gaps seen across socioeconomic levels and cultures.

The ideas presented as driving the common core may be simple in nature, but it is the perceived effects from the common standards and the way in which they are written that is superfluous to reform movement itself. Stating the standards are written to be more rigorous is an obtuse statement regarding the common core. Within these overall guidelines lies a focus on literacy and evidence based support for ideas that should cause an overall change in teaching methodologies (Gardner & Powell, 2013; Smith, Wilhelm, & Fredrickson, 2013). It must cause an overall change in teaching methodologies if these standards are to be implemented as written. Common Core standards set the stage for an upheaval in what teachers must do in the classroom. Across the curriculum, every adult in a classroom will have to shift their focus to include the basic tenants of reading and writing coherently while deriving information from text. These standards call for the mastery of complex vocabulary, high level analysis of text, comprehension of high level text, and even research based and scientific writing skills (Scruggs, Brigham, and Masteropieri, 2013). These are not generally a part of many classrooms outside of language arts and some social sciences.   The assumption appears to be that if a person can read and write effectively, then they can learn anything they need to learn more completely and more succinctly. To teach these things, the mindset of teachers, students, and parent must change. Common core, if implemented correctly, can cause that shift in ideology from the three major stakeholders in education.

Not written in the standards but just as likely as the necessary shift in teaching pedagogy as illustrated above, is the likelihood that teachers will be more proactive with their communication amongst peers as well as collaboration all across the United States. With the commonality in overall standards between 45 states and the school systems that reside within them, the amount of collaboration could be astounding. Most often, a teacher could look to the internet to find direction in lesson planning and activities for a specified unit they are teaching. That is with the many different standards for the thousands of school systems in the US. With common core, there could be endless lesson ideas and developments, as all of those teachers would be sharing and developing lessons for the same standards. The help for new teachers alone could make their transition into the field much smoother.   As many teachers improve on their lessons the more they implement them, more experienced teachers could share their lessons across the nation, speeding the improvement and transition into the common core's more rigorous standard of teaching and learning.

There are points against the implementation of the common core standards, though.   Perhaps the most stubborn is the idea that a localized education is necessary for people in different parts of the United States. The educational system was built on the foundations created in localized school systems to educate their populations. Education was not a power granted to the federal government, and as such, should be left up to the individual states and their local governments. This argument is mirrored in the opposition to NCLB. It is worth mentioning, that a generalized set of instructional methods and ideologies could be problematic for the very diverse populations which reside in different localities. A balanced must be reached between equality in outcome and specialized, localized education.

With regards to most reform movements and the changing of curricula, there is the great cost involved. Along with the new teaching methodologies that must accompany common core, is also the professional development to aid in the transition for teachers. In addition to the cost, there is researched based evidence that shows minimal effectiveness of professional development amongst the outcomes for students. Although teachers seemed to have increased their knowledge and understandings while also making appropriate transitions and changes to their classroom pedagogy, student performance shows minimal improvement (Loveless, 2013).

With each new curriculum and set of standards comes the need for new tests to measure the effectiveness of the outcomes for students. The design and implementation of those new systems is very costly and is a growing burden on the tax base with each necessary redesign. In addition to the costs and time it might take to create and implement new professional development and new tests, there is also the need for textbooks and other curriculum materials which match the new standards. The development of these products takes time and more money, while the standards are in place and teachers need materials immediately. In many ways, the entities that benefit the most from these reform movements are the companies that sell tests and textbooks.

Finally, with every new idea about what needs to be taught, there will certainly come a different point of view regarding the curriculum itself. With regards to common core, there are teachers and parents who disagree with the level of rigor and specificity for some age groups. With interest especially to the standards for K-5 students, some of the standards seem inordinately difficult for the developmental levels of those students. Some have called them completely unrealistic and impossible to implement (Yatvin, 2013). Many arguments in this arena, though, would likely come up for any redesign of standards.

Within many of these educational movements, there is a strong sense of equality. Multiple movements call for equality in experience, equality in access, and accountability in outcomes for all students. The desire to close the achievement gap between cultures and economic situations is strong. However, the way to do this is not to create strict standards with tests to measure them and rules to follow. The idea that government is holding teachers and systems accountable for closing the achievement gap is good hearted with a mindset in the right direction. However, it is generally obtuse to portray teachers as anything less than people who want the best for their students and for their schools. Just as any other profession, job, or toil, there are those who do their job well, those who get by, and those who are not appropriately placed in a job field. All people who do a job should be held accountable for that job. That is the reason there is leadership in any profession.

Accountability and teachers are not the problem. The epistemology at the heart of how teachers go about their business and what many believe constitutes an education is the issue. At the center of scientific argumentation based instruction, is the epistemological belief that students should create and construct knowledge for themselves. Meaning and understanding cannot be taught, they must be developed. I place at the heart of this, after many years in the classroom, the singular fact that a teacher can show and "teach" information but no one can understand it for a student. Constructivism is the heart of scientific argumentation as an instructional strategy. However it is more than a strategy, it is a wholesale philosophy that transfers across all curriculum area and applies to most everything in life. The ability to read and examine evidence and information, think critically, construct understandings and knowledge from evidence and information, take a stand in support of knowledge that has been constructed, defend that stance, rebut opposition, and ultimately comprehend thoroughly what you are doing is the result of implementing the methods of scientific argumentation.

Overall, I find it very difficult to be a great teacher of content without a basis in which you believe that learning takes place. In order to do that, you must have a conceptualization of what you believe knowledge to be and where you think it comes from. It is absolutely possible to be a good teacher, an effective teacher, or even a beloved teacher with no concern for the deeper philosophical questions regarding where knowledge or even the content you are teaching comes from. A friend once told me in my first year of teaching, that this job is 80% classroom management and 20% content knowledge. He felt as though if you had their attention and limited distractions then you could get across what you needed to get across. That served me well for many years until I started to wonder why I was not developing thinkers. In order to develop thinkers you must understand thinking and knowledge at a theoretical level. To design those lessons and activities that impart skills as well as knowledge and understanding, you must have a theory of what that is. This may not be a pristine and polished ideology, but there should be an epistemological basis to your instruction. Many of us developed a teaching philosophy in college and proceeded to tuck that away in a drawer at home or in a desk somewhere, never to be thought of again. I tell you right here and now, you need a theoretical understanding of what you do and what you teach.

As I examined some of the current movements in education that many complain about, myself included, with consistency I tried to point out specifically that a significant number of these movements have no epistemological heart and no scientific or research basis. Yet another plenty of them are recycled ideas that are not explained to teachers, parents, or students in a way that allows for the understanding of the epistemological or theoretical basis. Most people I know, whether personally or professionally, want to know why. If the only reason why is because someone somewhere tried it and it worked, or someone thought it out and it seemed like a good idea, then there is an issue. Education is about knowledge and understanding. Education should be about thinking, leaning, developing skills, and critical thinking. Those throughout history who have done great things have thought critically about situations, people, or the world around them and determined that there was an issue. Those who have created "the next great thing" have critically examined their world and determined that something was missing or something was underrepresented. These skills came through learning what they had to do and being involved in many different experiences. As we have molded education to a finite science, somewhere the theory was lost and the push for specificity created frameworks that were so specific there was no room for actually thinking.

Specific learning targets can be good if they are designed with the epistemological understanding that allows for teaching them in a way which encourages the same kind of thinking we assume went into developing those targets. Academic rigor is wonderful if the academics are rigorous in thinking and experiences that teach thinking. Accountability is wonderful if we understand what we are accountable for and those things are, once again, based in theory and an understanding of how and why the knowledge and understanding is created. To build background knowledge, to become critical thinkers, and to creatively approach new and different situations, we need experience in doing just that. More experience, and thinking about that experience, is still at its heart one of the only theoretically and epistemologically based educational methodologies that has been proven through experience and research. Project and problem based learning is a good start to a resurgence of these methodologies. However, the more I see this in practice, the clearer it is to me that teachers without that theoretical understanding of what they are doing are still struggling to implement activities that reach the specific learning goals in PBL's theoretical basis. Here I will try and relate a methodology that has a sound theoretical bases (I provide that basis as well) and works to mold experiences and build a critical thinking and experiential basis for students to take with them into the rest of their lives which allows for democratic thinking, social efficiency, and social mobility where applicable.

Appendix: Teaching Materials

Scientific Argumentation-Based Lab Debrief

As you approach any laboratory activity, you should focus on what you can learn about the physics involved through the activity. Activities are performed in physics class for the purpose of inquiring about the scientific laws and theories we are learning. As such, this should be the directions your attention goes.

You will construct a scientific argument based on the lab activity performed. Remember that a scientific argument used specific

Claim: Looking at what you did in the lab, what we are studying in class, and what the data show, you can develop an idea or some understandings that you can show to be true.

Claim:

_____

_____

_____

_____

_____

_____

_____

Data/Evidence: This is data that you collected specifically from this lab that supports the assertion you are making as your claim. This is the data that will prove your claim and is likely the evidence that you used to actually decide on a claim. This data should be displayed in a table, chart, or graph.

Data:

Reasoning: This is an explanation as to why the data supports and proves the claim. Here, specific connections explain what the claim means and the knowledge that has been developed. After explaining the reasoning, there should be no question as to how the data relates to the claim, how the claim and data relate to the lab, and how the claim and data relate to scientific understanding. There should be a clear explanation as to why the data and conclusions are legitimate. This may include what care was taken in the lab to make sure that the data was accurate and conclusive.

Reasoning:

_____

_____

_____

_____

_____

_____

_____

_____

_____

_____

_____

_____

Counterargument: This is where it is determined what another's argument might be either against the ideas developed in the lab or another's argument which explains the data with a different claim. Counterarguments may include concepts such as human error or other scientific theory as an explanation for lab results.

Counterargument:

_____

_____

_____

_____

_____

_____

_____

_____

_____

Rebuttal: A rebuttal is the original arguer's opportunity to discredit or disprove the counterargument. Here, the arguer can focus on why the counterargument is not correct, why there is not enough data to support the counterargument, and/or why the counterargument has not correctly applied scientific theory or law.

_____

_____

_____

_____

_____

_____

_____

_____

Constructing a Claim

What ideas or position on the subject matter at hand have you developed?
What position or idea will you be arguing in favor of or against?

What are the conditions that your claim is true in? Are there times that your claim is not true or reasonable? Write down any situational or case specific requirements of your claim here. (This is uncommon)

Can your claim be supported by evidence, data, examples and fact or theory in the field? If so list a few examples.

Are there other claims that can also be made that are similar to yours? Are there claims that are different than yours? What are they?

How can you state your claim so that it is very clear and precise? Will people reading or listening to your claim be very clear about what you are saying? Have you been specific? Write your Claim as specific and precise as possible here. Be sure to use field appropriate language and vocabulary.

Name _____ Period_____ Date _____

Get Your Evidence Together Organizer

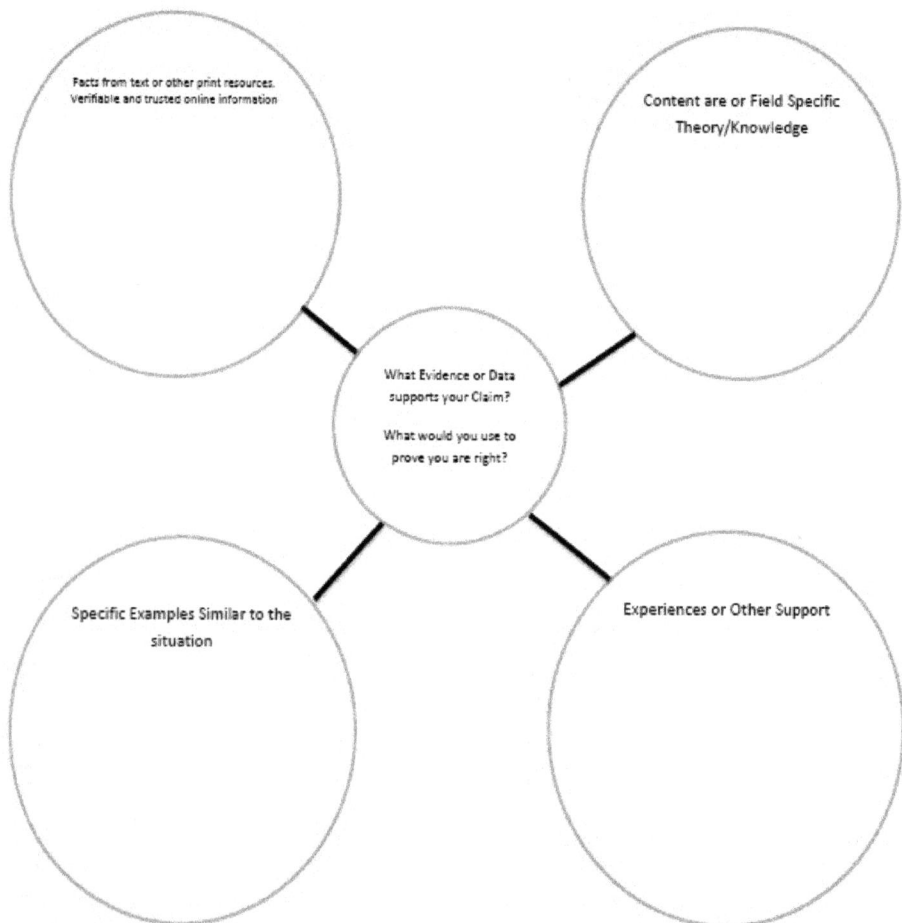

Facts from text or other print resources.
Verifiable and trusted online information

Content are or Field Specific
Theory/Knowledge

What Evidence or Data
supports your Claim?

What would you use to
prove you are right?

Specific Examples Similar to the
situation

Experiences or Other Support

Name _____ Period _____ Date_____

So What? What are the reasons your Evidence and Data Prove your Claim?

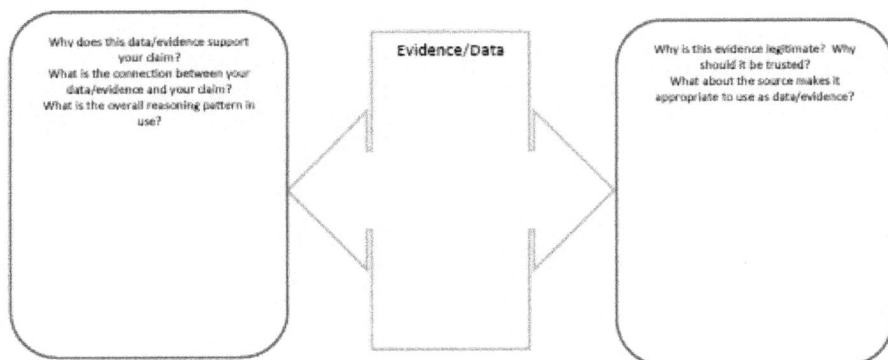

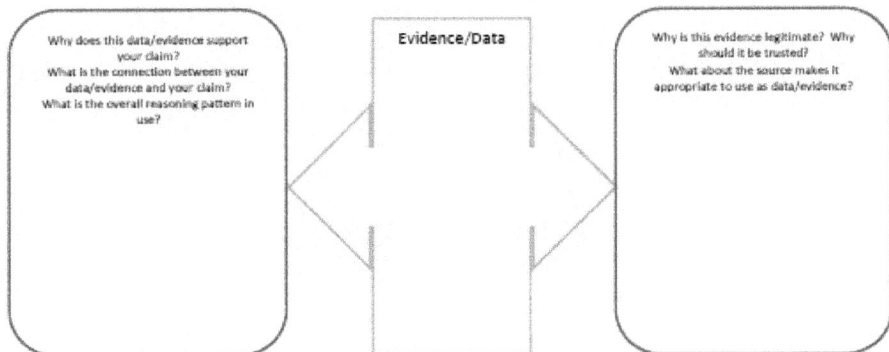

Why does this data/evidence support your claim? What is the connection between your data/evidence and your claim? What is the overall reasoning pattern in use?	Evidence/Data	Why is this evidence legitimate? Why should it be trusted? What about the source makes it appropriate to use as data/evidence?

Why does this data/evidence support your claim? What is the connection between your data/evidence and your claim? What is the overall reasoning pattern in use?	Evidence/Data	Why is this evidence legitimate? Why should it be trusted? What about the source makes it appropriate to use as data/evidence?

Why does this data/evidence support your claim? What is the connection between your data/evidence and your claim? What is the overall reasoning pattern in use?	Evidence/Data	Why is this evidence legitimate? Why should it be trusted? What about the source makes it appropriate to use as data/evidence?

An Alternate Assessment of the situation: The Counterargument

The counterargument is an alternate claim, data/evidence, and reasoning pattern which attempts to explain the same thing that you are attempting to explain. In to fully solidify an argument, you must also examine alternate proposals or possibilities.

What is an alternate point of view to my claim? What claim can be made from this point of view that offers an alternate explanation/theory to mine?	
What date/evidence is there which supports this alternate claim?	Why might someone believe the alternate point of view for the subject matter? What reasoning might connect the data/evidence to the alternate claim?

The Rebuttal: What is wrong with the Counterargument?

List the counterargument to your claim

| |
| |

What can you find wrong with the data/evidence, the legitimacy of that evidence, or the reasoning used to connect the data/evidence to the counterclaim?

Data/Evidence	
Why is it not legitimate?	Why is it not accurate or applicable?
What is the reasoning connecting this evidence to the claim?	
Why is the reasoning not warranted?	

Data/Evidence	
Why is it not legitimate?	Why is it not accurate or applicable?
What is the reasoning connecting this evidence to the claim?	
Why is the reasoning not warranted?	

Data/Evidence	
Why is it not legitimate?	Why is it not accurate or applicable?
What is the reasoning connecting this evidence to the claim?	
Why is the reasoning not warranted?	

Part of Argument	Description	Questions to ask yourself	Your Argument
Claim/qualifiers	This is your argument. What are you trying to prove or convince someone of? Make this statement clear and precise. This is where you state any qualifying situations in which your claim is or is not true.	What am I trying to prove? What am I saying is the correct answer or explanation? What am I saying is the right idea or interpretation? Is my claim true all of the time? Is my claim is true in certain situations or not true in certain situations.	
Data/Evidence	This is the data that you are using to support your claim. This can also be referred to as the evidence that you have to show that your claim is correct or the right idea to consider	What facts did I consider when deciding on my claim? What evidence will convince others that a) I am right? What facts/evidence supports my claim?	
Legitimacy	This is where you prove that your evidence should be trusted and is authentic. You must show your data/evidence to be from legitimate sources and factually based.	Why is this data/evidence assuredly facts that can be used in this specific field? Are my sources experts? Are my sources and facts accepted in the field I am examining?	
Reasoning	This is where you show why your data/evidence supports your claim. You are making the connections and showing why the evidence supports your thinking. AND....You are also citing field theory or concepts that prove that your evidence does indeed back up your claim.	Why does my evidence support my claim? What is the connection between my evidence and my claim? Why should your evidence be believed as support for your claim? What scientific theory supports the connections that I have made between my evidence and my claim?	
Counterargument	This is where you think of positions or claims that others may have against your argument. This is how you determine what someone who doesn't agree with you might believe. This is where you determine why others might have a different opinion	What is an alternate point of view to my claim? Why might someone believe the alternate point of view for the subject matter? What evidence might someone give to support an alternate claim?	
Rebuttal	This is how you convince others who hold opposing view that your view is correct. This is how you show that opposing points of view are invalid or incorrect. This is where you show why opposing evidence is invalid or does not support opposing claims	Why are alternate views not correct? What evidence shows that my claim is more valid or more correct than the alternate claims? Why is the evidence supporting alternate views incorrect? Why is the science supporting alternate views not appropriate to support those claims?	

Evaluating Peer Arguments

Name _____ Period _____ Date _____

Part of Argument	1 Poor Quality or not present	2 Needs improvement	3 Less than Average	4 Good Quality	5 Excellent Quality	Score
Claim	No claim present	claim has nothing to do with subject matter	Claim is not clear	Claim is clear and explains what it is support of	Claim is clear and precise as it explains what it is support of	
Evidence	No evidence is provided	Evidence is provided but does not support the claim	Some evidence is provided which does support the claim.	Most evidence that supports the claim is provided.	All evidence that can be used to support the claim is provided.	
Legitimacy	Evidence is not from legitimate sources	No legitimacy for evidence is provided	Little legitimacy for evidence is provided	Some legitimacy for evidence is provided	Thorough legitimacy for evidence is provided	
Quality of Evidence	No evidence is present	There may be data or an example but both are not present	There is at least one citation of data and one example given in support of the claim. Some scientific theory is used as evidence	There is at least one citation of data and one example given in support of the claim. Some scientific theory is used as evidence	There is multiple citations odd data, examples, and full scientific theory is used as evidence	
Reasoning	No reasoning is provided	Reasoning is provided but does not connect the data to the claim	Evidence is connected to the claim	Evidence is connected to the claim and there is an explanation as to why the evidence supports the claim based on the facts presented.	Evidence is clearly and precisely connected to the claim and there is a clear explanation as to why the evidence supports the claim based on the facts provided as well as all applicable scientific theory related to the situation	
Counterargument	There is no attention paid to a counterargument	A counterargument is noted, but it does not apply to the situation	A counterargument has been identified	Counterarguments have been identified and explained	All counterarguments have been identified and explained	
Rebuttal	There is no rebuttal for the counterargument	A rebuttal has been identified but does not apply to the counterargument	A rebuttal has been identified and applies to the counterargument described	A rebuttal which applies to counterarguments identified and explained	Rebuttals that apply to all counterarguments have been identified and explained	

Resources

Albe, V. (2008). When scientific knowledge, daily life experience, epistemological and social considerations intersect: students' argumentation in group discussions on a socio-scientific issue. *Research in Science Education*, 38(1), 67-90.

Andrews, R. (1995). *Teaching and learning argument*. London. New York: Cassell.

Arvola, A., & Lundegard, I. (2012). "It's her body" when students' argumentation shows displacement of content in a science classroom. *Research in Science Education*, 42(6), 1121-1145.

Ayla, G., & Filiz, K. (2010). WCES-2010: Designing and evaluating a specific teaching intervention on chemical changes based on the notion of argumentation in science. *Procedia - Social and Behavioral Sciences*, 2(Innovation and Creativity in Education), 1214-1218.

Becker, C. (2010). American education discourse: language, values, and U.S. federal policy. Journal for Critical Education Policy Studies (JCEPS), 8(1), 409-446.

Bell, P., & Linn, M. C. (2000). Scientific arguments as learning artifacts: designing for learning from the web with KIE. *International Journal of Science Education*, 22(8), 797-817.

Bell, S. (2010). Project-Based Learning for the 21st Century: Skills for the Future. Clearing House: A Journal of Educational Strategies, Issues and Ideas, 83(2), 39-43.

Berland, L., & Reiser, B. J. (2009). Making sense of argumentation and explanation. *Science Education*, 93(1), 26-55.

Bottcher, F., & Meisert, A. (2011). Argumentation in science education: a model-based framework. *Science & Education*, 20(2), 103-140.

Bulgren, J., Ellis, J., & Marquis, J. (2013). The use and effectiveness of an argumentation and evaluation intervention in science classes. *Journal of Science Education and Technology, (serial online)*. June 2013.

Carbonaro, W., & Covay, E. (2010). School sector and student achievement in the era of standards based reforms. Sociology of Education, 83(2), 160-182

Castells, M., Enciso, J., Cerveró, J. M., López, P., & Cabellos, M. (2007). What can we learn from a study of argumentation in the students answers and group discussion to open physics problems?. In

Pinto, R and Couso, D (Eds.). Contributions from Science Education Research.

Cavagnetto, A. R. (2010). Argument to foster scientific literacy: a review of argument interventions in k-12 science contexts. *Review of Educational Research*, (3), 336.

Chin, C., & Osborne, J. (2010). Students' questions and discursive interaction: their impact on argumentation during collaborative group discussions in science. *Journal of Research in Science Teaching*, 47(7), 883-908.

Chin, C., & Osborne, J. (2010). Supporting argumentation through students' questions: case studies in science classrooms. *Journal of the Learning Sciences*, 19(2), 230-284.

Chin, C., & Teou, L. (2009). Using concept cartoons in formative assessment: scaffolding students' argumentation. *International Journal of Science Education*, 31(10), 1307-1332.

Choi, A., Notebaert, A., Diaz, J., & Hand, B. (2010). Examining arguments generated by year 5, 7, and 10 students in science classrooms. *Research in Science Education*, 40(2), 149-169.

Christ, T. W. (2014). Scientific-based research and randomized controlled trials, the "gold" standard? Alternative paradigms and mixed methodologies. *Qualitative Inquiry, 20*(1), 72-80.

Clark, D. B., D'Angelo, C. M., & Menekse, M. (2009). Initial structuring of online discussions to improve learning and argumentation: incorporating students' own explanations as seed comments versus an augmented-preset approach to seeding discussions. *Journal of Science Education and Technology,* (4), 321.

Clark, D. B., & Sampson, V. (2008). Assessing dialogic argumentation in online environments to relate structure, grounds, and conceptual quality. *Journal of Research in Science Teaching,* 45(3), 293-321.

Clary, R., & Wandersee, J. (2013). Arguing history. *Science Teacher,* 80(5), 39-43.

Cobb, P. P. (1994). Constructivism in mathematics and science education. *Educational Researcher,* 23(7), 4.

Corbin, J. M., & Strauss, A. L. (2008). *Basics of qualitative research: techniques and procedures for developing grounded theory.* Los Angeles: SAGE Publications.

Corinne, Z. (2007). The development of scientific thinking skills in elementary and middle school. *Developmental Review*, (2) 172-223.

Costello, P. J. M., & Mitchell, S. (1995). *Competing and consensual voices: The theory and practice of argument*. Clevedon; Philadelphia: Multilingual Matters.

Costrell, R. M., & Betts, J. R. (2001). Incentives and Equity under Standards-based Reform. Brookings Papers on Education Policy, (1), 9.

Cross, D., Taasoobshirazi, G., Hendricks, S., & Hickey, D. T. (2008). Argumentation: a strategy for improving achievement and revealing scientific identities. *International Journal of Science Education,* 30(6), 837-861.

Denzin, N and Lincoln, Y (Eds.) (1994). *Handbook of qualitative research.* Thousand Oaks, CA US: Sage Publications, Inc.

Dewey, J. (1938),(1998). *Experience and education. 60ᵗʰ anniversary edition.* Indianapolis, Indiana: Kappa Delta Pi.

Dewey, J. (1933). *How we think, a restatement of the relation of reflective thinking to the educative process*. Boston, New York: Heath and company.

Dewey, J. *My pedagogic creed*. School Journal vol. 54 (January 1897), pp. 77-80.

Dewey, J. (1956). *The child and the curriculum and the school and society*. Chicago: University of Chicago Press

Dewey, J. (1929), (1984). *The later works, 1925-1953: The quest for certainty.* Carbondale: Southern Illinois University Press.

Driver, R., Asoko, H., Leach, J., Mortimer, E., & Scott, P. (1994). Constructing scientific knowledge in the classroom. *Educational Researcher*, (7), 5.

Duschl, R. (2007). Quality argumentation and epistemic criteria. In Erduran, S., & Aleixandre, M. (2008). *Argumentation in science education: Perspectives from classroom-based research*. Dordrecht: Springer.

Duschl, R. A., & Osborne, J. (2002). Supporting and promoting argumentation discourse in science education. *Studies in Science Education*, 3839-72.

Ebru, K., Sibel, E., & Pinar Seda, C. (2012). Discourse, argumentation, and science lessons: match or mismatch in high school students' perceptions and understanding? Mevlana *International Journal of Education*, (3), 1.

Eichhorn, D. H. (1969). Middle school--promise of the future.

Eichhorn, D. H. (1973). Middle school in the making. Educational Leadership, 31(3), 195-197.

English, M. C., & Kitsantas, A. (2013). Supporting student self-regulated learning in problem- and project-based learning. The Interdisciplinary Journal of Problem-Based Learning, 7(2), 128-150.

Erduran, S. (2007). Breaking the law: promoting domain-specificity in chemical education in the context of arguing about the periodic law. *Foundations of Chemistry*, 9(3), 247-263.

Erduran, S., & Aleixandre, M. (2008). *Argumentation in science education: Perspectives from classroom-based research*. Dordrecht: Springer.

Erduran, S., Ardac, D., & Yakmaci-Guzel, B. (2006). Learning to teach argumentation: Case studies of pre-service secondary science teachers. *Eurasia Journal of Mathematics, Science & Technology Education*, 2(2), 1-14.

Erduran, S., & Dagher, Z. R. (2007). Exemplary teaching of argumentation: a case study of two science teachers. In, Pintó, R., Couso, D. (Eds). *Contributions from Science Education Research*. (p. 403).

Echevarria, J., Short, D., & Powers, K. (2006). School reform and standards-based education: a model for english-language learners. Journal of Educational Research, 99(4), 195-210

Felton, M. (2004). The development of discourse strategies in adolescent argumentation. *Cognitive Development*, 19(1), 35-52.

Felton, M., & Kuhn, D. (2001). The development of argumentive discourse skill. *Discourse Processes*, 32(2-3), 135-153.

Fensham, P. J. (1988). *Development and dilemmas in science education*. London; New York: Falmer Press.

Ford, M. (2008). Disciplinary authority and accountability in scientific practice and. *Science Education*, 92(3), 404-423.

Foucault, M., & Gordon, C. (1980). *Power/knowledge: Selected interviews and other writings, 1972-1977.* New York, N.Y.: Pantheon Books.

Gardner, N. S., & Powell, R. (2013). The Common Core is a change for the better. The Phi Delta Kappan, (4). 49.

Gott, R. R., & Duggan, S. S. (2007). A framework for practical work in science and scientific literacy through argumentation. *Research in Science & Technological Education*, 25(3), 271-291.

Granger D. (2003). Positivism, skepticism, and the attractions of "paltry empiricism": Stanley Cavell and the current standards movement in education. Philosophy of Education Yearbook [serial online]. January: 146-154

Hand, B., Wallace, C., & Yang, E. (2004). Using a science writing heuristic to enhance learning outcomes from laboratory activities in seventh-grade science: quantitative and qualitative aspects. research report. *International Journal of Science Education*, 26(2), 131-149.

Hess, F. M., & McShane, M. Q. (2013). Common Core in the real world. The Phi Delta Kappan, (3). 61.

Hewson, M. G., & Ogunniyi, M. B. (2011). Argumentation-teaching as a method to introduce indigenous knowledge into science classrooms: opportunities and challenges. *Cultural Studies of Science Education*, 6(3), 679-692.

Hinn, C. A., & Brewer, W. F. (1993). The role of anomalous data in knowledge acquisition: a theoretical framework and implications for science instruction. *Review of Educational Research*, (1), 1.

Hogan, K., & Maglienti, M. (2001). Comparing the epistemological underpinnings of students' and scientists' reasoning about conclusions. *Journal of Research in Science Teaching*, 38(6), 663-687.

Homer-Dixon, T. F., & Karapin, R. S. (1989). Graphical argument analysis: a new approach to understanding arguments, applied to a debate about the window of vulnerability. *International Studies Quarterly*, 33(4), 389.

Hovey, K. A., & Ferguson, S. L. (2014). Chapter 6: teacher perspectives and experiences: using project-based learning with exceptional and diverse students. Curriculum & Teaching Dialogue, 16(1/2), 77-90.

Howard M. G. (2011). Arguing separate but equal: a study of argumentation in public single-sex science classes in the United States. *International Journal of Gender, Science and Technology*, (1), 70.

Hudicourt-Barnes, J. (2003). The use of argumentation in Haitian Creole science classrooms. *Harvard Educational Review*, 73(1), 73-93.

Hynd, C., & Alvermann, D. E. (1986). The role of refutation text in overcoming difficulty with science concepts. *Journal of Reading*, (5), 440. In Jimenez-Aleixandre (Eds.), *Argumentation in science education: perspectives from classroom-based research*. Dordrecht: Springer.

Jackson, R. (2008). Pedagogues, periodicals, and paranoia. Society, 45(1), 20-29.

Jiménez-Aleixandre, M., & Erduran, S. (2008). Argumentation in science education: an overview. *Argumentation in science education: perspectives from classroom-based research*. Dordrecht: Springer. (p. 3-25).

Jimenez-Aleixandre, M., & Pereiro-Munoz, C. (2002). Knowledge producers or knowledge consumers? argumentation and decision making about environmental management. *International Journal of Science Education*, 24(11), 1171-90.

Jimenez-Aleixandre, M., Rodriguez, A., & Duschl, R. A. (2000). "Doing the lesson" or "doing science": argument in high school genetics. *Science Education*, 84(6), 757-92.

Kelly, G. J., & Bazerman, C. C. (2003). How students argue scientific claims: a rhetorical-semantic analysis. *Applied Linguistics* -Oxford-, 2428-55.

Kelly, G. J., & Chen, C. (1999). The sound of music: constructing science as sociocultural practices through oral and written discourse. *Journal of Research in Science Teaching*, 36(8), 883-915.

Kelly, G. J., Chen, C., & Prothero, W. (2000). The epistemological framing of a discipline: writing science in university oceanography. *Journal of Research in Science Teaching,* 37(7), 691-718.

Kelly, G. J., Druker, S., & Chen, C. (1998). Students' reasoning about electricity: combining performance assessments with argumentation analysis. *International Journal of Science Education*, 20(7), 849.

Kelly, G. J., & Takao, A. (2002). Epistemic levels in argument: an analysis of university oceanography students' use of evidence in writing. *Science Education*, 86(3), 314-342.

Keys, C. W., Hand, B., Prain, V., & Collins, S. (1999). Using the science writing heuristic as a tool for learning from laboratory investigations in secondary science. *Journal of Research in Science Teaching*, 36(10), 1065-84.

Khishfe, R. (2012). Relationship between nature of science understandings and argumentation skills: a role for counterargument and contextual factors. *Journal of Research in Science Teaching*, 49(4), 489-514.

Kind, P., Kind, V., Hofstein, A., & Wilson, J. (2011). Peer argumentation in the school science laboratory-exploring effects of task features. *International Journal of Science Education*, 33(18), 2527-2558.

Kolsto, S. (2006). Patterns in students' argumentation confronted with a risk-focused socio-scientific issue. *International Journal of Science Education*, 28(14), 1689-1716.

Kornhaber, M. L., Griffith, K., & Tyler, A. (2014). It's not education by zip code anymore--but what is it? conceptions of equity under the common core. Education Policy Analysis Archives, 22(4),

Kuhn, D. (2001). How Do people know? Psychological Science, (1), 1

Kuhn, D. (2010). Teaching and learning science as argument. *Science Education*, 94(5), 810-824.

Kuhn, D. (1991). *The skills of argument*. Cambridge; New York: Cambridge University Press.

Kuhn, D., & Crowell, A. (2011). Dialogic argumentation as a vehicle for developing young adolescents' thinking. *Psychological Science*, (4), 545.

Kuhn, D., Shaw, V., & Felton, M. (1997). Effects of dyadic interaction on argumentative reasoning. *Cognition and Instruction*, 15(3), 287-315.

Kuhn, D., & Udell, W. (2003). The development of argument skills. *Child Development*, (5), 1245.

Kuhn, D. (2010). Teaching and learning science as argument. Science Education, 94(5), 810-824.

Kuhn, D. Wang, Y. & Li, H. (2011). Why argue? developing understanding of the purposes and values of argumentative discourse. *Discourse Processes*, 48(1), 26-49.

Kuhn, T. (1962). *The structure of scientific revolutions.* Chicago: University of Chicago Press.

Labaree, D. F. (2011). Targeting Teachers. Dissent, (3), 9.

Labaree, D. F. (2012). School syndrome: Understanding the USA's magical belief that schooling can somehow improve society, promote access, and preserve advantage. Journal of Curriculum Studies, 44(2), 143-163.

Labaree,D.F,, Hirsch Jr., E.D, (2004), Barbara beatty brookings papers on education policy, No. 7 pp. 89-129

Labaree, D. F. (1997). Public goods, private goods: the American struggle over educational goals. American Educational Research Journal, (1). 39.

Labaree, D. F. (1999). The chronic failure of curriculum reform. Education Week, 18(36), 42.

Labaree. D.F. (1997) American Educational Research Journal Vol. 34, No. 1 pp. 39-81

Labaree, D. F. (2000). Resisting educational standards. The Phi Delta Kappan, (1). 28.

Labaree, D. F. (2011). The lure of statistics for educational researchers. Educational Theory, 61(6), 621-632.

Labaree, D. F. (2011). Consuming the public school. Educational Theory, 61(4), 381-394.

Laguardia, A., & Pearl, A. (2009). Necessary educational reform for the 2lst century: the future of public schools in our democracy. Urban Review, 41(4), 352-368.

Lam, S., Cheng, R. W., & Ma, W. K. (2009). Teacher and student intrinsic motivation in project-based learning. Instructional Science, (6). 565

Latour, B. (1987). *Science in action: how to follow scientists and engineers through society.* Cambridge, Mass: Harvard University Press.

Lawson, A. E. (2003). The nature and development of hypothetico-predictive argumentation with implications for science teaching. *International Journal of Science Education*, 25(11), 1387-1408.

Lattimer, H., & Riordan, R. (2011). Project-based learning engages students in meaningful work: students at high tech middle engage in project-based learning. Middle School Journal, (2). 18.

Lee, J. S., Blackwell, S., Drake, J., & Moran, K. A. (2014). Taking a leap of faith: redefining teaching and learning in higher education through project- based learning. Interdisciplinary Journal of Problem-Based Learning, 8(2), 1-17.

Lemke, J. L. (1990). *Talking science: Language, learning, and values*. Norwood, N.J.: Ablex Pub. Corp.

Levy, F., Murnane, R. J., & Levy, F. (2001). Will standards-based reforms improve the education of students of color? National Tax Journal, 54(2), 401-15.

Loui, R. (2005). A citation-based reflection on Toulmin and argument. *Argumentation: An International Journal in Reasoning*, 19(3), 259-266.

Loveless, T. (2013). The Common Core Initiative: What Are the Chances of Success? Educational Leadership, 70(4), 60-63.

Lubienski, S. T. (2004). Traditional or standards-based mathematics? the choices of students and parents in one district. Journal of Curriculum and Supervision, 19(4), 338-365.

Luera G, Otto C. (2005). Development and evaluation of an inquiry-based elementary science teacher education program reflecting current reform movements. Journal of Science Teacher Education [serial online].16(3):241-258.

Malone, B. G., & Nelson, J. S. (2006). Standards-Based reform: panacea for the twenty-first century? Educational Horizons, 84(2), 121-128

Maloney, J., & Simon, S. (2006). Mapping children's discussions of evidence in science to assess collaboration and argumentation. *International Journal of Science Education*, 28(15), 1817-1841.

Mason, L. (1998). Sharing cognition to construct scientific knowledge in school context: the role of oral and written discourse. *Instructional Science*, 26(5), 359-89.

Mason, J. (2002). *Qualitative researching*. London; Thousand Oaks, California: Sage Publications.

McNeill, K. L. (2009). Teachers' use of curriculum to support students in writing scientific arguments to explain phenomena. *Science Education*, 93(2), 233-268.

Newton, P., Driver, R., & Osborne, J. (1999). The place of argumentation in the pedagogy of school science. *International Journal of Science Education*, 21(5), 553-76.

Newton, P., Driver, R., & Osborne, J. (2000). Establishing the norms of scientific argumentation in classrooms. *Science Education*, 84 (3), 287-312.

Nickerson, R. (1986). *Reflections on reasoning*. Hillsdale, N.J.: L. Erlbaum Associates

Nielsen, J. (2013). Dialectical features of students' argumentation: a critical review of argumentation studies in science education. *Research in Science Education*, 43(1), 371-393.

Osborne, J. (2010). Arguing to learn in science: The role of collaborative, critical discourse. *Science*, 328(5977), 463-466.

Osborne, J., Erduran, S., & Simon, S. (2004). Enhancing the quality of argumentation in school science. *Journal of Research in Science Teaching*, 41(10), 994-1020.

Parker W, Camicia S. (2009). Cognitive praxis in today's "international education" movement: a case study of intents and affinities. Theory & Research in Social Education [serial online]. Winter; 37(1):42-74.

Patronis, T., Potari, D., & Spiliotopoulou, V. (1999). Students' argumentation in decision-making on a socio-scientific issue: implications for teaching. *International Journal of Science Education*, 21(7), 745-54.

Pennycook, J. (2011). Education reforms and cautionary tales. Our Schools / Our Selves, 20(2), 125-139.

Piaget, J. (1952). *The origins of intelligence in children.* New York: International Universities Press.

Piaget, J., & Inhelder, B. (2000). *The psychology of the child.* New York: Basic Books.

Pontecorvo, C., & Girardet, H. (1993). Arguing and reasoning in understanding historical topics. *Cognition and Instruction*, (3/4), 365.

Prasad, P. (2005). *Crafting qualitative research: working in the postpositivist traditions.* Armonk, N.Y.: M.E. Sharpe.

Qhobela, M. (2012). Using argumentation as a strategy of promotion of talking science in a physics classroom: what are some of the challenges? Online Submission (serial online). January 1, 2012.

Reed, C., & Rowe, G. (2005). Translating toulmin diagrams: theory neutrality in argument representation. *Argumentation: An International Journal on Reasoning*, 19(3), 267-286.

Rubin, H., & Rubin, I. (2005). *Qualitative interviewing: The art of hearing data (2nd ed.)*. Thousand Oaks, Calif.: Sage Publications.

Ruggieri, C. A. (2003). Speaking my mind: rethinking standards-based reform. English Journal, 92(4), 15-17.

Sadler, T. D. (2006). Promoting discourse and argumentation in science teacher education. *Journal of Science Teacher Education*, 17(4), 323-346.

Sadler, T. D., & Donnelly, L. A. (2007). Socioscientific argumentation: the effects of content knowledge and morality. *International Journal of Science Education*, 28(12), 1463-1488.

Sampson, V., & Blanchard, M. R. (2012). Science teachers and scientific argumentation: trends in views and practice. *Journal of Research in Science Teaching*, 49(9), 1122-1148.

Sampson, V., & Clark, D. (2009). The impact of collaboration on the outcomes of scientific argumentation. *Science Education*, 93(3), 448-484.

Sampson, V., & Clark, D. B. (2008). Assessment of the ways students generate arguments in science education: current perspectives and recommendations for future directions. *Science Education*, 92(3), 447-472.

Sandoval, W. & Reiser, B. (2004). Explanation-driven inquiry: integrating conceptual and epistemic scaffolds for scientific inquiry. *Science Education*, 88(3), 345-372.

Sandoval, W. A., & Millwood, K. A. (2005). The quality of students' use of evidence in written scientific explanations. *Cognition and Instruction*, (1), 23.

Schulenberg, J. L. (2007). Analysing police decision-making: assessing the application of a mixed-method/mixed-model research design. *International Journal of Social Research Methodology, 10*(2), 99-119.

Schwarz, B., Neuman, Y., Gil, J., & Ilya, M. (2003). Construction of collective and individual knowledge in argumentative activity. *The Journal of the Learning Sciences*, (2), 219.

Scott, P. (1998). Teacher talk and meaning making in science classrooms: a vygotskian analysis and review. *Studies in Science Education*, 32(1), 45.

Scott, T. (2011). A nation at risk to win the future: the state of public education in the U.S. Journal for Critical Education Policy Studies (JCEPS), 9(1), 267-316.

Scruggs, T. E., Brigham, F. J., & Mastropieri, M. A. (2013). Common core science standards: implications for students with learning disabilities. Learning Disabilities Research & Practice, 28(1), 49-57.

Simon, S., Erduran, S., & Osborne, J. (2006). Learning to teach argumentation: research and development in the science classroom. *International Journal of Science Education*, 28(2-3), 235-260.

Simon, S., Johnson, S., Cavell, S., & Parsons, T. (2012). Promoting argumentation in primary science contexts: an analysis of students' interactions in formal and informal learning environments. *Journal of Computer Assisted Learning*, 28(5), 440-453.

Simonneaux, L. (2001). Role-play or debate to promote students' argumentation and justification on an issue in animal transgenesis. *International Journal of Science Education*, 23(9) 903-928.

Skerrett, A. (2008). Racializing educational change: Melting pot and mosaic influences on educational policy and practice. Journal of Educational Change, 9(3), 261-280.

Smith, M. W., Wilhelm, J. D., & Fredricksen, J. (2013). The common core: new standards, new teaching. The Phi Delta Kappan, (8). 45.

Takao, A., Prothero, W., & Kelly, G. (2002). Applying argumentation analysis to assess the quality of university oceanography students' scientific writing. *Journal of Geoscience Education*, 50(1), 40-48.

Tamim, S. R., & Grant, M. M. (2013). Definitions and uses: Case study of teachers implementing project-based learning. The Interdisciplinary Journal of Problem-Based Learning, 7(2), 72-101

Tippett, C. (2009). Argumentation: the language of science. *Journal of Elementary Science Education*, 21(1), 17-25.

Thomas, J. W. (2000). A review of PBL. Retrieved March 3, 2010, from http://www.bie.org/research/study/review_of_project_based_learning _2000/

Toulmin, S. (2003). The uses of argument (Updated ed.). Cambridge, U.K.; New York: Cambridge University Press.

Tseng, K., Chang, C., Lou, S., & Chen, W. (2013). Attitudes towards Science, Technology, Engineering and Mathematics (STEM) in a Project-Based Learning (PjBL) Environment. International Journal of Technology and Design Education, 23(1), 87-102.

Verheij, B. (2003). Artificial argument assistants for defeasible argumentation. *Artificial Intelligence*, 150(1/2), 291.

Verheij, B. (2005). Evaluating arguments based on Toulmin's scheme. *Argumentation: An International Journal on Reasoning*, 19(3), 347-371.

Vinson, K. D. (2001). Image, authenticity, and the collective good: The Problematics of Standards-Based Reform. Theory & Research in Social Education, 29(2), 363-374.

Von Aufschnaiter, C., Erduran, S., Osborne, J., & Simon, S. (2008). Arguing to learn and learning to argue: case studies of how students' argumentation relates to their scientific knowledge. *Journal of Research in Science Teaching*, 45(1), 101-131.

Voss, J., & Van Dyke, J. (2001). Argumentation in psychology: background comments. *Discourse Processes*, 32 (2&3), 89-112.

Vygotskiĭ, L, Cole, M. (transl) (1978). *Mind in society: The development of higher psychological processes*. Cambridge: Harvard University Press.

Vygotskiĭ, L, & Hanfmann, E. (transl.) (1962). Thought and language. Cambridge: M.I.T. Press, Massachusetts Institute of Technology.

Vygotsky, L. (1981). The instrumental method in psychology. In J. V. Wertsch (Ed.), The concept of activity in Soviet psychology (pp.134-144). Armonk, NY: M.E. Sharpe.

Walton, D. (1989). Dialogue theory for critical thinking. Argumentation, 3(2), 169-184.

Walton, D. (1996). Argumentation schemes for presumptive reasoning. Mahwah, NJ: Erlbaum

Walton, D. N. (2006). *Fundamentals of critical argumentation*. Cambridge [UK]; New York: Cambridge University Press.

Wellington, J. J., & Osborne, J. (2001). *Language and literacy in science education*.

Buckingham; Philadelphia, PA: Open University Press.

Wertz, F. J. (2011). *Five ways of doing qualitative analysis: phenomenological psychology, grounded theory, discourse analysis, narrative research, and intuitive inquiry*. New York, NY: Guilford Press.

Wilson, C., Taylor, J., Kowalski, S., & Carlson, J. (2010). The relative effects and equity of inquiry-based and commonplace science teaching on students' knowledge, reasoning, and argumentation. *Journal of Research in Science Teaching*, 47(3), 276-301.

Winegar, L. T., & Valsiner, J. (1992). *Children's development within social context*. Hillsdale, N.J.: L. Erlbaum.

Yatvin, J. (2013). Warning: The Common Core standards may be harmful to children. The Phi Delta Kappan, (6). 42.

Zohar, A., & Nemet, F. (2002). Fostering students' knowledge and argumentation skills through dilemmas in human genetics. *Journal of Research in Science Teaching*, 39 (1), 35-62.